Nicky,

THANKS for your time and TLC!

Happy mincing!

Nancy

Defending dignity. Fighting poverty.

CARE is an international humanitarian aid organisation fighting global poverty, with a special focus on working with women and girls to bring lasting change in their communities. We are non-religious and non-political, working together with communities to provide emergency relief and address the underlying causes of poverty.

Every day, in more than 20 of the poorest countries in the world, CARE Australia helps women, their families and communities transform their lives through our poverty-fighting and disaster-relief programs.

In many of the poorest countries in the world, women and girls are most affected by poverty.

Millions of women can't access vital health services, get an education, earn an income or join in community decision making. When you think about it, this means literally half of the knowledge, talent and strength in poor communities is being wasted.

That's why CARE is focusing on empowering women worldwide. We're building and supporting schools that teach girls alongside boys. We're providing women with small loans so they can turn their talents into businesses. We're introducing community projects where men and women work together to accomplish what had seemed impossible.

At CARE, we've found that women and girls have enormous potential to fight poverty and create positive change with far-reaching effects.

We seek a world where every person has the opportunity to realise their potential because, in the end, that's the key to truly ending injustice and poverty:

One woman.
One family.
One community at a time.

She has the power to change her world. You have the power to help her do it.

To donate:
1800 DONATE | www.careaustralia.org.au/donatenow | SMS 0437 37 CARE

This book is dedicated to my mother

whose cooking was the making of legends

and to my husband

whose support has been just as legendary.

Published in Australia 2009 by Nancy Chan-Bennett
Edited by: Elspeth Parker
Typeset by: Nicky Szychter
Cover design by: Dan Bolton
Pre-Press and print production 3E Innovative Pty Ltd www.3e.net.au

Text copyright © Nancy Chan-Bennett 2009

ISBN 978-0-646-51991-3

The moral right of the author has been asserted

Acknowledgements

I am deeply indebted to many of my friends who have given me invaluable support to get this book published. These include those who provided me with free publishing and legal advice, those who shared with me their recipe ideas, those who willingly tested recipes on their families, those who were forthcoming with sweet words of encouragement, and those who expended considerable time and energy on copy-editing, type-setting and cover design.

I also owe a great deal to my family (Mick, Emma and Luke) for placing their trust and belief in me, and for blithely eating virtually nothing but mince in the last eight months.

Contents

Other Starters and Main Meals - Asia

Other Starters and Main Meals - Middle East & Africa

Other Starters and Main Meals - Europe & The Americas

Introduction

How I decided to go on a mince journey?

Some time ago, my 12 year-old son who adores food and all things sweet said to me, in a rather patronising tone, "Mum, you shouldn't eat to live, you should live to eat". "Mate, I'm Chinese – haven't you noticed?" I retorted. I wouldn't go so far as to say that my love of food is genetically pre-programmed. But my formative years were spent in Hong Kong where food bordered on being a religion – a fact that my precocious son had conveniently overlooked.

Prior to undertaking any research or planning for this book, I must admit that my passion for food did not carry me as far as mince. Like most people, I'd dismissed it (rather too readily) as a 'humble staple'. It went into my supermarket trolley dutifully every week but I never strayed beyond the traditional favourites of spaghetti bolognese or chilli beef – until some time in late 2008, when I finally tired of that familiar feeling of *'not-the-same-thing-again'*, and wished for something new and exciting. I reached into the dim, dark recesses of my memory but struck blank. Further time spent time fossicking through a clutter of old magazine cuttings was equally fruitless. It yielded little and was a wasted effort. My instincts told me that there had to be many, many delectable recipes on mince but they were scattered all over, and someone had to find them and put them all in the one place.

It did not take me long to conclude that that someone had to be me, and that a book on mince is the obvious place to house some, if not all of these brilliant recipes. It sounded fun when I laid out the scope of the project – trawling for recipe ideas on the Internet and in public libraries, testing and developing them, and writing them up afterwards. All that sounded pleasurable enough but I had no idea of what was in store.

What happened in the eight months that followed was somewhat akin to a magical, mystery tour! It was packed with marvellous surprises, and I was left in awe and wonderment at the richness of my find.

I found innovative ways of cooking traditional favourites which yielded superb results – an example of this was the cottage pie with cauliflower instead of potatoes (see page 130). I encountered gorgeous recipe ideas for pasta and risotto using crumbled Italian sausages, and came upon Asian recipes that captured the quintessence of stir-fries – quick, fresh and scrumptious.

Last but not least, I discovered the vast array of ingredients you could add to meatballs to give them:

- different tastes – fresh herbs (e.g. coriander, mint and dill), fresh and dried fruit (e.g. red apples, currants and cranberries), spices (e.g. cumin, paprika and cinnamon) and cheeses (e.g. Parmesan and ricotta);

  and

- different textures, e.g. whipped egg whites for an airy texture, and breadcrumbs soaked in milk/cream for a melt-in-the-mouth feel;

It has been a wonderful, culinary journey for me with each new recipe idea the offer of a different adventure! I sincerely hope you can join me on some of these adventures, and be touched by some of the magic – there truly is nothing 'humble' about mince!

The benefits of mince

First and foremost, **everyone loves it!** And I'm not just talking about kids or baby-boomers. It is big on flavour and a taste sensation in its own right. It marries beautifully with herbs and spices, and combines so well with other ingredients to give complexities in tastes and textures. Think luscious meatballs with grated red apples, exquisite kofta with currants and pine nuts and heavenly fried rice with minced beef and lettuce! No wonder it is adored by one and all!

It's so versatile – You know you can always create a great meal using mince. This makes it a 'must-have' on your shopping list, particularly when you're on the weekly treadmill of planning Monday-to-Friday meals for the family.

It's economical – A consideration that cannot be brushed aside in times of economic uncertainty. (Do you know that you can make restaurant-standard risotto for the family for as little as $12?)

It's everywhere – It is stocked by many retailers, from gigantic supermarkets in mega malls to your local stores around the corner.

It gets you out of a tight spot – If your household is anything like mine, and you have commitment-shy young adults, or visitors who become ring-in dinner guests, then mince is a 'god-send'. You can always bulk it up and make it stretch to address the needs of the moment.

It's a shape-shifter – You can pack it firmly to make a rissole, have it loosely thrown together in a sauce, or scatter it through a mountain of fried rice.

What kind of mince recipes are included in this book?

Recipes that are mouth-watering. They will have your loved ones begging for more. I've cooked and tested all the recipes, and feedback from family and friends have invariably ranged from good to terrific!

Recipes with ingredients that are readily available. It is hard enough juggling the demands of everyday living without having to go through the angst of hunting down unusual ingredients for your meals.

Recipes with different flavours and styles that mirror our contemporary, multi-cultural society. Whenever we eat out, we are presented with a myriad of choices by way of restaurants (Chinese, Thai, Italian, etc.). We can enjoy this same luxury of choice when cooking mince from recipes originated from all around the world.

Some recipes may deviate slightly from traditional methods of preparation. However, we live in an age of fusion cooking, and national cuisines around the world are ever-evolving to reflect changes in tastes and eating habits

What kind of mince recipes are excluded from this book?

For the sake of a healthier heart, I've resisted the temptation to include deep-fried recipes, however appealing.

Which grades of mince to use?

Fat content is the factor that distinguishes between different grades of mince – the higher the grade, the lower the amount of fat it contains. There is not much difference in tenderness but grades with more fat are well suited for barbecuing as they do not dry out as easily, and thus demand less vigilance from the cook.

Leaner grades are preferred by those who are more health-conscious as they are much easier on the heart and cholesterol levels. They also taste much better when eaten cold.

If possible, try and go for the leaner grades particularly when cooking pork and lamb as these are fattier meats than chicken or beef.

If you have a food processor or meat grinder, you can easily make your own mince and assume perfect control over the fat content. It also saves you the hassle of going around different stores looking for a specific kind of mince as some types (e.g. veal, pork or lamb) are not always available.

Things you'd like to know about meatballs, rissoles and patties

Meatballs, rissoles and patties have long delighted the hearts and stomachs of diners young and old. They absorb the flavours of herbs and spices brilliantly, and are easy to eat. They are also very versatile. You can make them into any shape or size. (Feel free to deviate from the shapes or sizes specified in the recipes but make sure you adjust cooking times accordingly.)

You can serve meatballs as finger food at a big party or dish them up as a family fare with mash and veggies. If you're serving them cold (for instance, at a picnic), remember to drain and absorb the oil with paper towels after frying. You may not notice the thin film of oil clinging to the meat when it is piping hot but once it cools down, it will be a different story.

Meatballs or rissoles/patties?

Meatballs are great in soups, stews and sauces whereas rissoles and patties are good for grilling, barbecuing and pan-frying. Their flatter shape makes them cook through quickly without drying out or burning. Rissoles are generally bigger than meatballs but smaller than patties. They can be oval and flat, or round like giant-sized meatballs. Of course, the bigger the meatballs or rissoles/patties, the longer they take to cook. But then, they are more of a time-saver to make than the smaller ones!

Breadcrumbs or not?

The jury seems to be out on this one. Some chefs avoid adding breadcrumbs because they tone down the hearty, meaty taste, (and I did subscribe to this thinking before embarking on this 'mincing' adventure). Other chefs favour breadcrumbs and see them as having the dual benefits of:

- making the meat tender;
- keeping the meat moist particularly when mixed in with a small amount of water, wine, milk or cream.

I must admit that after tasting meatballs with bread/breadcrumbs soaked in milk or wine, I've become a total convert! It's such a simple addition, and yet they have the power to transform mere morsels of meat into plump and juicy meatballs that are irresistible! Of course, breadcrumbs also act as a filler and make the meat go further which is very handy when you have drop-in dinner guests!

While it is economical and convenient, try to avoid pre-packaged breadcrumbs off the supermarket shelves. You can make fresh breadcrumbs by blitzing day-old bread in a blender/food processor or a spice/meat grinder. Failing that, you might want to buy breadcrumbs from bakeries or specialty grocers, and store them in the freezer—ready for use at a moment's notice.

The right amount of seasoning?

People vary a great deal in the level of seasoning they like. This explains why it is unspecified in many recipes. As a rough guide only, add about ¼ to ½ teaspoon of salt to 500g of meat. Add less if other ingredients with high salt content (e.g. Parmesan cheese, Dijon mustard and soy sauce) are included. Add more, if there is a fair amount of breadcrumbs, milk or fresh herbs in the meat mixture or if you're going to serve your meatballs cold. If you're unsure, test it by frying a small lump of meat mixture in a pan – then taste and adjust.

Combining and kneading

It is important to combine all ingredients well, and often the best way to do this is to use your hands. If you're put off by the idea of handling mince with your hands, try using food gloves or even a plastic freezer bag. (It may not do as good a job but it works!) Some recipes, particularly those with added liquid, require kneading. Kneading has the effect of binding, and of working the 'wet' ingredients into the dry. In Middle Eastern and some Asian cuisines, kneading is essential as it helps to create a tight-knit, spongy texture that is highly prized.

I would like to highlight the fact that while some recipes call for kneading, others (such as the Italian ones) caution specifically against doing this. When lightness in texture is required, over-working the meat mixture would spoil the result. In those instances, you should mix until all ingredients are just combined – and no more.

Whenever you find the meat mixture too sticky to handle comfortably (e.g. this typically happens when you've ground the meat in a food processor), try wetting your hands in cold water. Then shake off any excess, and rub your palms together for a few times.

Refrigeration

Refrigerating meat mixtures for 30 minutes or more has the benefit of making them firmer, and easier to shape into meatballs or patties/rissoles.

If you've made your meatballs, patties/rissoles in advance and stored them in the refrigerator, don't forget to take them out half an hour before you cook them. It takes the chill out of the meat and will give a better result.

Soups

Chinese West Lake beef soup

This classic Chinese soup is named after the West Lake in Hangzhou which is renowned for its breath-taking beauty. It is easy to make and yet rich with flavours.

300g minced beef

1 litre (4 cups) chicken stock

½ tsp sugar

salt and white pepper

1 tbsp corn flour dissolved in 2 tbsp water

2 egg whites, lightly beaten

1-2 tbsp fresh coriander leaves, chopped

For the marinade:

1 tbsp light soy sauce (or regular soy)

1 tbsp Chinese rice wine (or dry sherry)

1 tbsp water

2 tsp corn flour

sprinkling of sesame oil

Combine minced beef with marinade, and allow to stand for 10 minutes or more.

In a large pot, add stock and bring to a boil. Add marinated beef, and stir to break up any lumps. Bring to a boil again, and add sugar. Reduce heat to low. Cover and simmer for a few minutes. Then season with salt and pepper.

Stir in corn flour/water mixture, and cook until the soup boils and thickens slightly.

Remove from heat. Gradually drizzle in egg whites, stirring in one direction until they form short threads. Sprinkle with coriander, and serve immediately. ***Serves 3-4***

Handy tips

Meat: beef

How about .. serving it with steamed rice either on the side or mixed in with the soup as a simple but satisfying meal. You may wish to add ½ a cup of green peas if you're serving this as a one-bowl meal.

Macanese meatball soup with vermicelli

The Macanese cuisine is from Macau, a former Portuguese colony on the South China coast, and is an exotic mix of east and west. Serve these noodles as a one-pot meal at the weekend, and watch your family wolf it down!

1 litre (4 cups) beef or chicken stock	For the meatballs:
1-2 tbsp vegetable oil	**500g minced beef, pork or chicken**
2-3 tbsp fresh mint leaves, roughly chopped	**1 tsp corn flour**
	2 spring onions, finely chopped
250g dried rice vermicelli noodles	**1 egg white**
4 hard boiled eggs, chopped	**¼ tsp salt (or to taste)**
150g (1 cup) frozen green peas, cooked	**generous sprinkling of white pepper**

To make the meatballs, combine all ingredients. Mix well with your hands, and shape tablespoons of meat mixture into balls.

In a pan, bring stock to a boil. Add oil, and drop meatballs gently into the stock. Cover and cook for 5-6 minutes or until meatballs are done. Add mint leaves, and remove from heat.

In a separate pan, cook vermicelli in boiling water for 2 minutes, and drain well. Divide into 4 portions and put into pasta-sized bowls. In each bowl, put eggs and peas on top of the vermicelli. Then ladle meatballs and soup all over, and serve immediately. ***Serves 4***

Handy tips

Meat: beef / pork / chicken

How about .. serving it with rice stick noodles or egg noodles instead of vermicelli

Thai meatball and spinach broth

This clear, non-spicy, Thai soup can be served on its own or with rice. Fresh tofu (bean curd) makes a lovely addition, and is available from Asian grocery stores and select supermarkets. Rice with soup is extremely common across Asia and there seems to be at least two different ways of eating it. Some people like their rice on the side so that they can eat the 'solids' and drink the broth separately. Other people prefer ladling the soup onto the rice and eating them mixed together. The choice is yours entirely!

1 tbsp vegetable oil

4 garlic cloves, finely chopped

1.5 litres (6 cups) chicken stock (or ½ stock ½ water)

300g to 400g fresh tofu, cut into 2cm cubes

1 bunch (about 250g) English spinach, cut into 10cm lengths

2 spring onions, finely chopped

salt (to taste)

1 tbsp fresh coriander, finely chopped (to serve)

For the meatballs:

400g minced pork or chicken

2 tbsp fresh coriander, finely chopped

1-2 tbsp fish sauce (or soy sauce)

¼ tsp white pepper

To make the meatballs, combine all ingredients. Mix well, and shape into small balls.

In a small pan, heat oil over medium-low heat. Add garlic and stir-fry for several minutes until golden. Remove from pan. Drain on paper towels, and set aside.

In a large pot, bring stock to a boil. Reduce heat to medium, and drop in meatballs gently. Cover and cook for 3-4 minutes. Add tofu, and cook for another 4-5 minutes. (If you're using very lean pork, you might want to add a little oil). Toss in spinach and spring onions. Cook briefly for about 1 minute until the spinach is wilted. Add salt, then sprinkle with the fried garlic and coriander. Serve immediately. ***Serves 3-4***

Handy tips

Meat: pork / chicken

How about .. serving with rice or rice noodles

Persian meatball soup with rice

This Iranian recipe is great as a one-pot meal and is marvellous for those with a herb garden or who adore the fragrance of fresh herbs in their food. The mint and garlic garnish adds piquancy while the yoghurt gives it a refreshing touch.

2 tbsp vegetable oil

1 large onion, chopped

50g (¼ cup) yellow split peas

1 tbsp ground turmeric

1.25 litres (5 cups) water

¾ cup basmati (or long grain) rice

¼ cup fresh parsley, chopped

¼ cup fresh coriander, chopped

¼ cup spring onions (whites only), chopped

20g (1 tbsp) butter

1 large garlic clove, finely chopped

¼ cup fresh mint, chopped

2-3 saffron threads, soaked in 1 tbsp boiling water (optional)

plain yoghurt (to serve)

For the meatballs:

400g minced beef or lamb

1 large onion, grated

¼ tsp salt (or to taste)

black pepper

In a large pot, heat oil over medium-high heat, and fry onion until golden brown. Add split peas and turmeric, stir and fry briefly for 30 seconds. Pour in water, and bring to a boil before reducing heat to low. Cover and simmer for 20 minutes.

Make the meatballs by combining all ingredients. Mix well, and shape into small balls. Drop meatballs gently into the pan, and continue to simmer for another 10 minutes.

Then add rice, parsley, coriander and spring onions. Mix well. Simmer further for about 30 minutes, or until the rice is cooked. Stir from time to time to prevent from sticking.

Meanwhile, in a small pan, heat butter over medium heat and fry garlic until golden. Add mint, and fry briefly for about 30 seconds. Sprinkle mint-garlic mixture and saffron liquid (if using) over the soup. Ladle into 4-5 soup bowls, and serve each topped with a spoonful of yoghurt. ***Serves 4-5***

> ### *Handy tips*
> **Meat**: beef / lamb
>
> **How about** .. serving it with some pita bread on the side

Middle Eastern meatball soup with lemon and eggs

The combination of lemon and eggs in a broth or soup is found in many different guises throughout the Middle East. This recipe is a hearty soup with the tanginess of lemon giving a fine counterbalance.

2 tbsp vegetable oil

1 large onion, chopped

100g (½ cup) yellow split peas

3 tsp ground turmeric

1 litre (4 cups) chicken/beef stock or water (or ½ stock, ½ water)

1 bunch (about 250g) spinach, chopped

juice of 1-2 lemons

salt and black pepper

4 eggs, lightly beaten

For the meatballs:

400g lean minced lamb, chicken or beef

1 onion, grated

1-2 garlic cloves, crushed

2 tbsp flat-leaf parsley, finely chopped

¼ tspn salt (or to taste)

black pepper

In a large pot, heat oil over medium-high heat, and fry onion until golden brown. Add split peas and turmeric, and fry very briefly for 30 seconds. Pour in stock, and bring to a boil before reducing heat to low. Cover and simmer for 20 minutes.

Make the meatballs by combining all ingredients. Mix well, and shape into small balls. Drop meatballs gently into the pan, and continue to simmer for another 10 minutes.

Add spinach, and simmer for 15 more minutes. Stir in half the lemon juice, and season with salt and pepper. Simmer for a further 15 minutes.

Remove soup from heat, and stir in eggs. Adjust seasoning to taste, and add remaining lemon juice, if necessary. *Serves 4-5*

Handy tips

Meat: lamb / chicken / beef

How about .. serving it with pita or Turkish bread on the side

Middle Eastern soup with tomato and couscous

Here's a satisfying soup that can be easily turned into a meal on its own—just add more couscous (½ or ¾ a cup). It's particularly comforting on a cold, winter evening, and while the list of ingredients may seem long, it's really easy once you've done all the chopping!

1 tbsp vegetable oil	1 litre (4 cups) chicken stock
1 celery stalk, chopped	1 x 400g tin chopped tomatoes
1 carrot, chopped	1 tbsp fresh coriander, chopped
1 onion, chopped	1 tbsp fresh mint, chopped
1 large garlic clove, crushed	1 tbsp flat-leaf parsley, chopped
1 tsp ground coriander	1-2 tbsp fresh lemon juice
1 tsp ground cumin	salt (to taste)
¼-½ tsp cayenne pepper (optional)	70g (⅓ cup) instant couscous
200g lean minced lamb	plain yoghurt (to serve - optional)

Heat oil in a large pot over medium heat, and fry celery, carrot, onion and garlic until vegetables soften. Add ground coriander, cumin and cayenne (if using), and fry very briefly for 30 seconds. Add minced lamb, and fry for a few minutes until meat slightly browns, stirring to break up any lumps. Add stock and tomatoes. Bring to a boil before turning heat to low. (Skim the surface of the soup with a spoon, if necessary.) Cover and simmer for 30-40 minutes.

Handy tips

Meat: lamb

How about .. serving it with pita or Turkish bread

Add fresh coriander, mint, parsley, lemon juice and salt. Finish by adding couscous before removing from heat. Allow to stand for 3-4 minutes. Mix well, and serve topped with a dollop of yoghurt (if using). ***Serves 4***

Pasta and meatball soup

This is a rustic, Italian dish of plump meatballs and garden vegetables served in a pasta soup thickened with pureed cannellini beans. Choose pasta shapes that are hollow so that they can scoop up the delicious soup as you eat.

1 x 400g tin cannellini beans, drained and rinsed

1 litre (4 cups) vegetable or beef stock (or ½ stock, ½ water)

2 tbsp olive oil

2 celery stalks, finely chopped

1 carrot, finely chopped

1 onion, finely chopped

2 garlic cloves, finely chopped

1 tbsp tomato paste

150g small, hollow pasta shapes (elbows, shells, macaroni, etc)

handful of basil leaves, torn

salt and black pepper

Parmesan cheese, grated (to serve)

For the meatballs:

1 slice sandwich bread (white or wholemeal)

60ml (¼ cup) milk

350g lean minced beef or veal

2 garlic cloves, crushed

2 tbsp fresh parsley, finely chopped

1 egg

¼ tsp salt (or to taste)

black pepper

To make the meatballs, soak bread in milk for about 10 minutes. Combine bread mixture with all other ingredients for meatballs, and mix well with your hands. (If the mixture appears too 'wet', knead it a little to enable the liquid to be absorbed). Shape into small balls.

> **Handy tips**
> **Meat**: beef/veal

Place cannellini beans with a little stock in a blender or food processor, and blend into a paste. In a large pot, heat oil over medium heat, and add celery, carrot, onion, and garlic. Fry vegetables for 4-5 minutes before reducing heat to low. Cover and simmer for another 5 minutes. Add bean puree, the remaining stock and tomato paste, and bring to a boil. Cover and simmer over gentle heat for 10 minutes.

Then add pasta, and simmer for 8-10 minutes or until pasta is tender, but not soft. Drop meatballs gently into the soup, and add basil. Cook for a further 8-10 minutes, then season with salt and pepper. Ladle into warmed soup bowls, and serve with grated Parmesan cheese. ***Serves 4***

Mixed bean and vegetable soup

This is a terrific recipe from my friend who's a foodie, and once ran a very successful catering business. It's packed with flavours and nutrition – and oh-so-easy!

1-2 tbsp vegetable oil	2 x 400g tins whole tomatoes
250g lean minced beef	500ml (2 cups) beef stock
1 carrot, chopped	salt and black pepper
1-2 celery stalks, chopped	1 x 400g tin cannellini beans, drained
1 onion, chopped	1 x 400g tin red kidney beans, drained
1 red capsicum, seeded and chopped	
½ tsp chilli powder (or to taste)	1-2 tbsp flat-leaf parsley, chopped

In a large pot, heat oil over medium heat. Fry minced beef, carrot, celery, onion and capsicum for several minutes until meat browns, taking care to break up any lumps. Add chilli powder, tomatoes and stock. Break up the tomatoes, and stir to mix well. Season with salt and pepper. Cover and simmer for 15-20 minutes.

Handy tips

Meat: beef

Add cannellini and red kidney beans, and simmer for a few minutes until heated through. Adjust seasoning to taste, if necessary. Sprinkle with parsley, and serve immediately with toast or crunchy bread. ***Serves 4-6***

Savoury Pastries

Curry puffs

Curry puffs are popular throughout Asia, and are ideal as snacks or starters! The filling in this recipe is Malaysian, and although fresh curry leaves are not available everywhere, it may be worthwhile to hunt them down because they do make a superb difference!

1 kg (6 sheets) of ready-rolled puff pastry (thawed before use)

1 egg, lightly beaten with water (to glaze)

For the filling:

2 tbsp Malay (or regular) curry powder

½ to 1 tsp chilli powder (optional)

2 tbsp vegetable oil

4 curry leaves (preferably fresh)

500g minced beef or chicken

1 large potato, diced

1 onion, finely chopped

1 tsp salt (or to taste)

pinch of sugar

Preheat oven to 200C (conventional), and grease a baking tray or line it with baking paper. To make the filling, combine curry powder and chilli powder (if using) with 1 tablespoon of water to make a paste. Heat oil in a pan, and stir-fry curry paste with curry leaves for a couple of minutes. Add minced meat, potato and onion. Stir-fry for 2-3 minutes, then add ½ cup of water. Cover and simmer over low heat until mixture is cooked and *dry*. Add salt and sugar, and stir to combine. Remove curry leaves from meat mixture, and set aside to cool.

On a lightly floured surface, lay out a pastry sheet. Cut out circles from the pastry using a cutter about 10cm in diameter. (If you don't have one, use a glass/cup of similar size.) Put a tablespoon of meat filling onto the centre of each pastry round. Dampen the edges with water, and fold one half over the other to make a half-moon shape. Seal by pressing the edges together. Then starting from one end, pinch small sections of this rounded border, and fold them back on each other to give a braided appearance.

Handy tips

Meat: beef / chicken

How about ..
serving them with a sweet chilli sauce. For a slightly different filling, try adding a diced carrot and/or ½-¼ cup green peas with the potato and onion

Repeat until all the meat filling is finished, re-rolling the pastry if necessary to cut out more rounds. Place on baking tray, and brush with egg glaze. Bake in pre-heated oven for 20 minutes or until pastry turns golden. ***Makes 20-24***

Thai-style mini sausage rolls

These sausage rolls are easy to make, and if you double the quantities, they will be fantastic as finger food on social occasions. I took them to a picnic with friends, and they were devoured within minutes!

335g (2 sheets) ready-rolled puff pastry (thawed before use)	**3 spring onions, chopped**
1 egg yolk, lightly beaten (to glaze)	**2 tbsp fresh coriander leaves, chopped**
2 tbsp sesame seeds	**1 tsp fresh ginger, chopped**
For the filling:	**1-2 small red chillies, chopped (optional)**
250g minced chicken or beef	**1 tsp fish sauce (or soy sauce)**
100g (2 rashers) bacon, chopped	**1 egg**
1 garlic clove, chopped	

Preheat oven to 180C (conventional), and grease a baking tray or line it with baking paper.

To make the filling, place all the ingredients in a food processor, and whiz until combined. (If you don't have a food processor, crush the garlic, grate the ginger, and chop bacon, spring onions, coriander and chillies finely. Then add fish sauce and egg, and mix thoroughly.)

Cut pastry sheets into halves. Take half a pastry sheet, and brush the two long edges with a little water. Take one-quarter of the filling, shape into a long sausage (using lightly floured hands), and place it along a long edge of the pastry. Fold over the pastry, and press down to seal. Trim away excess pastry. Repeat this process with the remaining filling and pastry.

> ### Handy tips
> **Meat**: chicken / beef
>
> **How about ..** serving them with sweet chilli sauce

Then with a very sharp knife, trim the two ends of the sausage rolls neatly. Place them with their sealed edges facing down, and cut into 4-5 cm lengths. Brush with egg glaze, and sprinkle with sesame seeds. Place on baking tray, and bake in pre-heated oven for 25-30 minutes or until meat is cooked through and the pastry is golden. ***Makes 20-24***

Samosas

In India, samosas are typically deep fried. In this recipe, however, they are brushed with oil and baked which makes them a slightly healthier alternative. They are great as an appetiser or a snack.

10-12 sheets (about 160g) filo pastry (if frozen - thaw before use)	**1 tbsp fresh ginger, grated**
	1 small red chilli (optional)
vegetable oil	**2 tsp garam masala**
For the filling:	**½ tsp ground turmeric**
1-2 tbsp vegetable oil	**300g minced lamb, beef or chicken**
1 onion, finely chopped	**150g (1 cup) frozen green peas**
1 tbsp fresh garlic, crushed	**salt (to taste)**

Preheat oven to 200C (conventional), and grease a baking tray or line it with baking paper.

To make the filling, heat oil over medium heat, and fry onion for several minutes until softened. Add garlic and ginger, and stir-fry briefly for a minute. Add chilli (if using), and stir in garam masala and turmeric. Add minced meat, and fry until browned, taking care to break up any lumps. Add peas, and fry briefly until they are cooked through. Season with salt, and set aside to cool.

> **Handy tips**
>
> **Meat**: lamb / beef / chicken
>
> **How about** ..
> serving them with tomato sauce or a sweet and sour chutney

Take a sheet of filo pastry, and cut into long strips of 9-10cm in width. Cover the rest of the pastry with a damp dish cloth to prevent from drying out. Brush the strip lightly with oil. Place a tablespoon of meat mixture at about 1 cm away from one end of the strip. Fold one corner over the meat mixture to make a triangular shape. Then fold this triangle over itself repeatedly until the meat mixture is sealed in and you've reached the end of the strip. Fold any edges over the triangle to make a neat, triangular shape. Repeat this process with the remaining filling and pastry.

Place samosas on baking tray in a single layer, and bake in pre-heated oven for about 15 minutes or until golden. Serve immediately. ***Makes 25-28***

Mini pastry pockets

These delicious morsels are ideal as finger food if you're entertaining! They are a little time-consuming because of the sheer number but they are not hard to make. The lovely filling in this recipe is typically Lebanese. Feel free, however, to substitute it with a filling of your choice.

670g (4 sheets) ready-rolled puff pastry (thawed before use)

1 egg, lightly beaten with a little water (to glaze)

For the filling:

55g (¹/₃ cup) pine nuts

400g minced lamb or beef (or ¹/₂ lamb, ¹/₂ beef)

1 small onion, grated

1 garlic clove, crushed

¹/₃ cup flat-leaf parsley, finely chopped

juice of ¹/₂ a lemon (or to taste)

¹/₂ tsp salt (or to taste)

black pepper

Preheat oven to 180C (conventional), and grease a baking tray or line it with baking paper.

To make the filling, dry roast the pine nuts in a frying-pan for about 30 seconds or until lightly golden. Add to all other ingredients, and mix well. (If you wish, taste and adjust seasoning by frying a small piece of meat mixture. This should taste a little saltier than your normal liking, but it'll be just right once it goes in with the pastry.)

> **Handy tips**
> **Meat**: lamb / beef

Take a sheet of pastry, and cut it into 5cm squares using a sharp knife and something with a straight edge. Keep the rest of the pastry covered to prevent from drying out. Take a square of pastry, and brush two opposite sides (left and right) lightly with the egg glaze. Place about half a teaspoon of meat mixture in the middle. Then fold the square in half by lifting the bottom right hand corner up to meet with the top right, and the bottom left with the top left. Pinch the corners and glazed sides to seal. Set it down *flat* on the work surface and you should have a pastry pocket with an opening filled with meat mixture facing upwards. Repeat this process with the remaining filling and pastry.

Place pastry pockets on baking tray in a single layer, and brush with egg glaze. Bake in pre-heated oven for about 30 minutes or until the meat is cooked through and the pastry is lightly golden. ***Makes 80-90***

Moroccan briouats

These enticing pastry snacks are from Morocco. The Moroccans serve them sprinkled with icing sugar and cinnamon, and while the combination may sound a little unusual, you'd be surprised at how well they go together!

8-10 sheets (about 130g) of filo pastry (if frozen, thaw before use)	**2 tbsp flat-leaf parsley, finely chopped**
40g (2 tbsp) butter, melted	**2 tbsp fresh coriander, finely chopped**
vegetable oil (for frying)	**400g minced lamb or beef**
icing sugar and ground cinnamon (to serve — optional)	**1 tsp ground coriander**
	½ tsp paprika
For the filling:	**generous pinch of ground ginger**
vegetable oil	**salt (to taste)**
1 onion, finely chopped	**2 eggs, lightly beaten**

To make the filling, heat a little oil in a non-stick frying pan over medium heat. Add onion, parsley and fresh coriander, and fry for several minutes until onion softens. Add minced meat and fry for a few minutes until *dry* and browned, taking care to break up any lumps. Drain off excess fat, if necessary. Add ground coriander, paprika, ground ginger and salt. Stir and cook for another minute. Remove from heat, and add eggs, stirring until they begin to set. Put aside to cool.

> **Handy tips**
>
> **Meat**: lamb / beef
>
> **How about ..**
> baking them instead in a pre-heated oven (190C conventional) for 15-20 minutes or until golden

Take a sheet of filo pastry, and cut into long strips of about 8cm in width. Cover the rest of the pastry with a damp dish cloth to prevent from drying out. Brush the strip lightly with melted butter. Place a heaped teaspoon of meat mixture at about 1 cm away from one end of the strip. Fold one corner over the meat mixture to make a triangular shape. Then fold this triangle over itself repeatedly until the meat mixture is sealed in and you've reached the end of the strip. Fold any edges over the triangle to make a neat, triangular shape. Repeat this process with the remaining filling and pastry.

Heat a little oil in a frying-pan, and fry briouats for 2-3 minutes each side until golden. Do not crowd the pan — fry in batches, if necessary. Drain on paper towels, and serve sprinkled with icing sugar and cinnamon (if using). *Makes 20-24*

Empanadas

There are countless variations (both sweet and savoury) of these crescent-shaped pasties. They are popular not only in Spain but in many other cuisines around the world that are Spanish-influenced (e.g. Mexico, the Caribbean and Latin America). The filling in this recipe is common in Argentina although I've opted for the commonly available puff pastry for ease of preparation.

500g (3 sheets) ready-rolled puff pastry (thawed before use)

1 egg, lightly beaten (to glaze)

For the filling:

1 medium potato

3 tbsp olive oil

1 small onion, finely chopped

2 garlic cloves, crushed

250g minced beef

2 tsp ground cumin

2 tsp paprika

salt and black pepper

2-3 tbsp green (or black) olives, pitted and sliced

2 hard-boiled eggs, chopped

Preheat oven to 200C (conventional), and grease a baking tray or line it with baking paper.

To make the filling, cook potato and dice into small (1cm) cubes. Fry in 1 tablespoon of oil over high heat for about a minute or so. Set aside to cool, and clean the pan. Over medium heat, fry onion in another tablespoon of oil until softened. Add garlic and fry for another 2-3 minutes. Remove from pan, and set aside.

Fry minced beef in the remaining tablespoon of oil until browned and dry, taking care to break up any lumps. Return onion/garlic mixture to the pan, and stir to mix well. Add cumin, paprika, and season with salt and pepper. Stir and cook for another couple of minutes. Remove from pan, and cool slightly. Add cooked potato, and mix gently.

> ### Handy tips
> **Meat**: beef
>
> **How about ..**
> using the Mexican picadillo (see page 133) as a filling, for variation

On a lightly floured surface, lay out a pastry sheet. Cut out circles from the pastry using a cutter about 10cm in diameter. (If you don't have one, use a glass/cup of similar size.) Put a tablespoon of beef mixture onto one half of a pastry round, taking care to leave a border all around. Put on top a few slices of olives and some chopped egg. Dampen the edges with water, and fold one half over the other to make a half-moon shape. Press the edges together with a fork to seal, and place on baking tray. Repeat until all the filling is finished, re-rolling the pastry if necessary to cut out more rounds.

Brush empanadas with egg glaze, and bake in pre-heated oven for 15-20 minutes, or until golden. ***Makes 14-16***

Spicy empanadas

This recipe for these crescent-shaped pasties hails from the Caribbean. It uses a scrumptious, home-made shortcrust pastry but if you're pressed for time, feel free to replace it with ready-made pastry from the supermarket.

2 egg yolks, lightly beaten (to glaze)

For the pastry:

250g butter or margarine

420g plain flour

2 tsp ground turmeric

1 tsp salt

5-6 tbsp ice-cold water

For the filling:

2 tbsp vegetable oil

1 onion, finely chopped

2 spring onions, finely chopped

2 garlic cloves, crushed

1-2 red or green chillies, seeded and finely chopped (optional)

350g minced beef

4 tomatoes, skinned and chopped

¼ tsp ground cardamom

¼ tsp ground cinnamon

¼ tsp ground cumin

¼ tsp ground ginger

¼ tsp ground turmeric

salt and black pepper

125ml (½ cup) water

Preheat oven to 200C (conventional), and grease a baking tray or line it with baking paper.

To make the pastry, cut the butter into thin 5cm pieces, and pulse together with the other ingredients in a food processor until the mixture resembles breadcrumbs. (If you don't have a food processor, soften the butter. Then mix it together with the other ingredients using your hands or a hand-held beater with fittings for dough.) Bring this crumbly mixture together into a dough with your hands. Don't over-work it or the pastry will turn hard and heavy. Wrap in cling wrap, and refrigerate for 1 hour.

Handy tips
Meat: beef

To make the filling, heat oil over medium heat, and fry onion for several minutes until softened. Add spring onions, garlic and chilli (if using), and fry for a couple more minutes. Add minced beef, tomatoes, spices, and season with salt and black pepper. Fry for a few minutes or until meat browns, taking care to break up any lumps. Add water, and reduce heat to low. Simmer, *uncovered,* for about 20 minutes or until mixture is *dry*. Remove from heat, and set aside to cool.

Sprinkle pastry lightly with flour, and roll it out between 2 pieces of cling wrap. (You may find it easier to do this in several smaller batches.) Cut out circles from the pastry using a cutter about 10cm in diameter. (If you don't have one, use a glass/cup of similar size.) Put a tablespoon of beef mixture onto one half of a pastry round, taking care to leave a border all around. Press the edges together with a fork to seal, and place on baking tray. Repeat until all the filling is finished, re-rolling the pastry if necessary to cut out more rounds.

Brush empanadas with egg glaze, and bake in pre-heated oven for 30 minutes, or until golden. ***Makes 20-24***

Easy meat and egg pie

Tasty yet easy – this makes a great lunch or light dinner. Just throw all the ingredients for the filling together, cover with a sheet of puff pastry and let the oven do all the work (45 minutes).

1 sheet ready-rolled puff pastry (thawed before use)

1 egg yolk, lightly beaten with a little water (to glaze)

For the filling:

400g minced beef or lamb

150g (3 rashers) bacon, finely chopped

1 medium onion, finely chopped

½ cup fresh parsley, finely chopped

125ml (½ cup) stock

2 tbsp plain flour

salt and black pepper

4 eggs

Preheat oven to 190C (conventional), and grease a baking dish or pie dish.

For the filling, combine all ingredients (except eggs). Spread meat mixture over the bottom of the baking/pie dish. Hollow out the filling in 4 places. Break eggs into the hollows. Prick yolks with a fork, and season eggs with salt and pepper.

> ### Handy tips
> **Meat**: beef / lamb
> **How about** ..
> serving with a green salad

Cover filling with the pastry sheet. Press the edges over (or into) the sides of the dish to seal. Trim surplus pastry and mark edges with a fork. Prick the top in several places and brush with egg yolk.

Bake in pre-heated oven for 15 minutes. Then reduce heat to 170C, and bake for a further 30 minutes or until pastry is golden. ***Serves 4***

Pasta

Pasta and meatballs stuffed with Fontina

Made with cubes of Fontina cheese in their centres, and flavoured with a hint of lemon and cinnamon, these meatballs are substantial in size and mouth-wateringly good! You can serve them with the simple tomato sauce below or use one of your own favourite recipes.

350g to 400g fettucine (or spaghetti)

Parmesan cheese, finely grated (to serve)

For the tomato sauce:

2 tbsp extra virgin olive oil

2-3 garlic cloves, finely chopped

1 x 400g tin chopped tomatoes

2 tbsp red or white wine

salt and freshly ground black pepper

For the meatballs:

250g lean minced beef

250g lean minced pork (or pork and veal)

25g (¼ cup) Parmesan cheese, finely grated

1 garlic clove, crushed

½ lemon, grated rind and juice

¼ tsp ground cinnamon

1 slice sandwich bread, crumbed (or ¼ cup dry breadcrumbs)

1 egg, lightly beaten

¼ tsp salt (or to taste)

freshly ground black pepper

80g Fontina cheese, cut into 8 cubes

dry breadcrumbs (for coating)

extra virgin olive oil (for frying)

Preheat oven to 180C (conventional), and line a baking tray with baking paper. To make the sauce, heat oil and fry garlic briefly for about 1 minute in a pan. Add tomatoes and wine, and season to taste with salt and pepper. Cover and simmer gently for about 20 minutes.

To make the meatballs, combine minced meats, Parmesan, garlic, lemon rind, lemon juice, cinnamon, breadcrumbs, egg and seasoning. Mix thoroughly using your hands. Shape into 8 balls. (You may wish to moisten your hands with cold water for easier handling of meat mixture.) Put each ball into your hand (in turn), and press a cube of Fontina into its *centre*. Reshape each ball, taking care to ensure that the cheese is centred and well covered. Then coat the meatballs in breadcrumbs,

Handy tips

Meat: beef & pork / veal

How about .. serving it with rice or potatoes instead of pasta

and fry them quickly in oil until lightly browned all over. Place on the lined baking tray, and bake in pre-heated oven for 20-25 minutes or until cooked through.

Cook pasta in a large pan of rapidly boiling salted water until *al dente*, and drain. Serve with meatballs topped with tomato sauce and a sprinkling of Parmesan.
Serves 3-4

Pasta with meatballs in red wine sauce

The sauce in this incredibly yummy recipe is rich in flavour and the meatballs literally melt in your mouth. Serve them to your family on a special occasion or invite some friends over to share. They'll all love you for it! Just make sure you buy the dry breadcrumbs from bakeries or specialty grocers.

350g to 400g pasta	1 egg
2 tbsp fresh parsley, finely chopped	½ tsp salt (or to taste)
Parmesan cheese, grated (to serve)	freshly ground black pepper
	extra butter (for frying)
For the meatballs:	
100ml (5 tbsp) red wine	For the red wine sauce:
60ml (¼ cup) thick (or double) cream	25g (2 tbsp) plain flour
6 tbsp dry breadcrumbs	250ml (1 cup) red wine
1 medium onion, finely chopped	250ml (1 cup) beef stock
20g (1 tbsp) butter	125ml (½ cup) thick (or double) cream
500g minced beef	
1 tbsp fresh chives, chopped (optional)	salt and freshly ground black pepper

To make the meatballs, mix wine with cream. Add breadcrumbs and allow to stand for 20 minutes or more. Over a gentle heat, fry onion in butter for 6-8 minutes until softened, and set aside to cool. Combine minced beef with wine/breadcrumb mixture, onion, chives (if using), egg, salt and pepper. Shape level tablespoons of meat mixture into balls.

In a frying-pan, (preferably non-stick), with a lid to fit, heat butter over medium heat. Fry meatballs quickly until lightly browned all over. Do not crowd the pan – fry in batches, if necessary. Remove from pan, and drain on paper towels.

> ### Handy tips
> **Meat**: beef
>
> **How about** .. serving it with potatoes instead of pasta

To make the sauce, turn heat to low and sprinkle flour into the pan you used to fry the meatballs. Stir the flour into the meat juices and fry briefly until it browns. Slowly add wine and stock, stirring constantly to combine and to prevent lumps from forming. Add cream and mix well. Season with salt and pepper. Cover and cook for 10 minutes. Then add meatballs and cook for another 30 minutes or so until the sauce thickens, turning meatballs over from time to time to coat evenly with sauce.

Cook pasta in a large pan of rapidly boiling, salted water until *al dente* and drain. Sprinkle parsley over meatballs and sauce. Serve with pasta and grated Parmesan. **Serves 4**

Carbonara with sausage meatballs

It's astounding the different things you can do with the 'humble' sausage! Here's a recipe that's quick, easy and an absolute delight.

600g good quality Italian pork sausages, skinned and crumbled	For the egg sauce:
extra virgin olive oil	**100ml (5 tbsp) thick (or double) cream**
2-3 rashers bacon, chopped	**4 egg yolks**
350g to 400g linguine (or spaghetti)	**50g (½ cup) Parmesan cheese, grated**
freshly ground black pepper and salt	
extra Parmesan cheese, grated (to serve)	**1 tbsp flat-leaf parsley, finely chopped**
	zest of ½ a lemon, grated

Roll sausage meat into balls of about 3-4 cm (in diameter). Heat oil in a frying-pan over medium heat. Fry meatballs until cooked through and browned all over. Do not crowd the pan – do this in batches, if necessary. Add bacon, and fry for several minutes until it crisps. Remove from pan, and set aside.

Cook pasta in a large pan of rapidly boiling salted water. Meanwhile, make the egg sauce by whipping up all the ingredients in a large bowl.

Handy tips

Meat: pork

When the pasta is *al dente*, drain and reserve a little of the cooking water. Return pasta to the pan, and immediately combine it with the sauce. Add meatballs and bacon, and toss gently to combine. If the pasta is too sticky, add a little of the reserved cooking water to loosen it up. Season with pepper and salt (if necessary). Serve immediately with extra Parmesan on the side. ***Serves 4***

Spaghetti with meatballs

Not surprisingly, there are many recipes for this all-time favourite. This beautiful one is from my friend of Italian origin who carries the recipe around in her head. The only change I've made is to speed up the cooking time for the sauce by using tomato passata instead of starting from scratch with tinned tomatoes.

350g to 400g spaghetti

Parmesan cheese, finely grated (to serve)

For the meatballs:

¼ cup dry breadcrumbs

500g minced beef, or pork and veal

25g (¼ cup) Parmesan cheese, finely grated (optional)

1 small onion, coarsely grated

1 large garlic clove, crushed

1-2 tbsp flat-leaf parsley, finely chopped

1 egg

salt and freshly ground black pepper

For the tomato sauce:

olive oil

1 onion, chopped

1-2 garlic cloves, crushed

400ml (1 ²/₃ cups) tomato passata (or pasta sauce)

125ml (½ cup) white/red wine, or stock

salt and black pepper

handful of basil leaves, torn

To make the meatballs, combine all ingredients and mix well with your hands. Shape level tablespoons of meat mixture into balls, and set aside.

To make the sauce, heat oil over medium heat. Add onion and garlic, and fry for a few minutes until onion softens. Add tomato passata and wine, and season with salt and pepper. Stir and mix to break up the tomatoes. Bring sauce to a boil before reducing heat. Cover and simmer for 25-30 minutes. Then drop meatballs gently into the sauce – a few at a time, allowing them to harden a little before adding more. Simmer for another 15-20 minutes, stirring gently once or twice to turn the meatballs over and coat them evenly with sauce. Gently stir in basil and remove from heat.

> **Handy tips**
> **Meat**: beef / pork / veal

Cook pasta in a large pan of rapidly boiling salted water until *al dente*, and drain. Serve with meatballs in tomato sauce and grated Parmesan. ***Serves 4***

Pastitccio

In Italy, pastitccio is made for special occasions, and is eaten as a main meal to be followed by a salad or vegetable course. Some recipes have it encrusted in pastry whereas others (like this one) do not. It does require a bit of work but your effort will be well rewarded.

250g macaroni (or penne)

75g (¾ cup) Parmesan cheese, grated

2 eggs, lightly beaten

2 tbsp dry breadcrumbs

For the meat sauce:

2 tbsp olive oil

2 onions, finely chopped

2 garlic cloves, finely chopped

600g minced beef

200g chicken livers, chopped (optional)

125ml (½ cup) beef stock

125ml (½ cup) dry white or red wine

1 x 400g tin whole tomatoes

⅓ cup tomato paste

1 tbsp fresh oregano, chopped

¼ tsp grated nutmeg

salt and freshly ground black pepper

1 egg

For the cheese sauce:

80g (4 tbsp) butter

75g (½ cup) plain flour

875ml (3½ cups) hot milk

100g (1 cup) Parmesan cheese, grated

2 egg yolks

Cook pasta in a large pan of rapidly boiling water until *al dente.* Drain and combine well with Parmesan and eggs. Spread pasta over the base of a greased, baking dish.

Preheat oven to 180C (conventional). To make the meat sauce, heat oil in a pan over medium heat. Fry onions and garlic for several minutes until onions soften. Add minced beef, and fry until browned, taking care to break up any lumps. Add chicken livers (if using), stock, wine, tomatoes, tomato paste, oregano and nutmeg. Stir to mix well, and season with salt and pepper. Bring sauce to a boil before reducing heat to low. Simmer gently, *uncovered,* for about 30 minutes or until mixture thickens. Set aside to cool, and then stir in egg.

Handy tips
Meat: beef

To make the cheese sauce, melt butter in a pan over medium heat. Add flour and stir for 1-2 minutes or until a smooth paste is formed. Remove from heat, and add hot milk gradually, stirring all the time to work the paste into the milk. Return to heat, and continue to stir until sauce boils and thickens. Stir in Parmesan, and set aside to cool for 5 minutes or so. Add egg yolks and mix well.

Spoon meat sauce onto cooked pasta in the baking dish. Pour cheese sauce on top and smooth surface with a spoon or knife. Finish with a sprinkling of breadcrumbs on top. Bake in pre-heated oven for about 1 hour, or until golden brown. Allow to stand for 10 minutes before serving. **_Serves 6_**

Lasagne with butternut pumpkin

In Italy, pumpkin is often teamed with pasta, and this fine combination is showcased here. Pasta sheets draped over the side of the baking dish create a stunning visual impact, and their crispiness makes them appetising as well. It's a truly impressive dish that will delight your friends!

1 butternut pumpkin, seeded and roughly chopped

olive oil

sea salt and freshly ground black pepper

8 fresh lasagne sheets

35g ($^1/_3$ cup) Parmesan cheese, grated

350g mozzarella, coarsely grated

For the meat sauce:

olive oil

150g pancetta (or bacon), finely chopped

pinch of cinnamon (optional)

1 large onion, finely chopped

1 carrot, finely chopped

3 garlic cloves, crushed

1-2 tbsp fresh oregano (or rosemary), chopped

500g minced beef

500g minced pork

2 x 400g tins whole tomatoes

250ml (1 cup) red wine

2 bay leaves

sea salt and freshly ground black pepper

For the béchamel sauce:

110g butter

110g (¾ cup) plain flour

1.25 litres (5 cups) hot milk

salt and white pepper

pinch of grated nutmeg (optional)

sea salt and freshly ground black pepper

To make the meat sauce, heat a little oil over high heat. Fry pancetta and cinnamon (if using) until pancetta crisps. Add onion, carrot, garlic and oregano, and fry for a minute. Add minced beef and pork, and cook for 5 minutes, taking care to break up any lumps. Then add tomatoes, wine and bay leaves. Bring sauce to a boil before reducing heat to low. Simmer, *uncovered,* for about 1½ hours. Then remove bay leaves, and season with salt and pepper.

Handy tips
Meat: beef & pork

Preheat oven to 180C (conventional). Rub pumpkin slices with oil, and sprinkle with salt and pepper. Place on a baking tray, and roast in pre-heated oven for the last 45 minutes of cooking the sauce. Remove from oven, and break into smaller pieces.

Increase oven temperature to 200C. Make the béchamel sauce by melting butter in a pan over medium heat. Add flour, and stir for 1-2 minutes or until a smooth paste is formed. Remove from heat, and add hot milk gradually, stirring all the time to work the paste into the milk. Return to heat, and continue to stir until sauce boils and thickens. Season with salt, pepper and nutmeg (if using).

To assemble the lasagne, oil a deep baking dish about 26cm x 35cm. Line the bottom with a layer of pasta sheets, and allow the pasta sheets to drape over the sides of the baking dish. Add a layer of meat sauce, a little béchamel sauce and a sprinkling of Parmesan. Then add a layer of pumpkin. Repeat this layering process until you finish with a layer of pasta covered in béchamel sauce. Sprinkle evenly on top with grated mozzarella and the remaining Parmesan. Cook in pre-heated oven for about 35-40 minutes until golden. Allow to stand for 10 minutes before serving. ***Serves 8***

Easy lasagne

In this easy recipe for lasagne, the meat sauce is flavoured with a lovely combination of beef (or veal) and succulent pork sausages, and it does not take long to cook. You don't even have to make a béchamel sauce – the white sauce is just a simple mix-and-stir!

olive oil	2 x 400g tins chopped tomatoes
6 fresh (or dried) lasagne sheets	salt and freshly ground black pepper
25g (¼ cup) Parmesan cheese, grated	For the white sauce:
150g mozzarella, roughly grated	500g ricotta
For the meat sauce:	50g (½ cup) Parmesan cheese, grated
olive oil	60ml (¼ cup) milk
1 medium onion, finely chopped	¼ cup flat-leaf parsley, finely chopped
2 garlic cloves, crushed	1 large egg, lightly beaten
400g minced beef or veal	pinch of grated nutmeg (optional)
250g Italian pork sausages, skinned and crumbled	salt and freshly ground black pepper

Preheat oven to 200C (conventional). To make the meat sauce, heat oil over medium-high heat. Fry onion for several minutes until golden. Add garlic and fry briefly for a minute. Add minced meat and sausage meat, and fry for 4-5 minutes until browned, taking care to break up any lumps. Add tomatoes, and season to taste with salt and pepper. Bring sauce to a simmering point. Simmer, *uncovered,* for about 30 minutes or until sauce thickens, stirring occasionally.

> **Handy tips**
> **Meat**: beef / veal & pork

To make the white sauce, combine all ingredients and mix well. To assemble the lasagne, brush an oval or rectangular baking dish with oil, and line the bottom with a layer of pasta. Add a layer of meat sauce, a little white sauce and a sprinkling of Parmesan. Repeat this layering process until you finish with a layer of pasta covered in white sauce. Sprinkle evenly on top with grated mozzarella and the remaining Parmesan. Cook in pre-heated oven for 30-35 minutes until golden, (allowing for extra cooking time if dried lasagne sheets are used). Allow to stand for 10 minutes before serving. ***Serves 6***

Tagliatelle with ragu Bolognese

This ragu recipe is delicious and rich! If you can afford the time, don't hurry the process – reducing the sauce slowly gives it that extra flavour. It's a very handy sauce to have in the freezer as it's an essential ingredient for so many other dishes (e.g. lasagne, cannelloni and cottage pie). So why not make twice the amount and keep half of it frozen for when you'd need it next! In Italy, this is served with tagliatelle but feel free to serve it with another type of long pasta.

120g pancetta (or rindless bacon), chopped	250g lean minced pork (or pork & veal)
20g (1 tbsp) butter	salt and freshly ground black pepper
1 tbsp olive oil	125ml (½ cup) dry white or red wine
1 onion, finely chopped	1 x 400g tin chopped tomatoes
1 carrot, finely chopped	250ml (1 cup) beef stock
1 celery stalk, finely chopped	60ml (¼ cup) thick (or double) cream
2 garlic cloves, crushed	350g to 400g tagliatelle
250g lean minced beef	Parmesan cheese, grated (to serve)

Over a medium heat, fry pancetta in butter and oil until it crisps. Add onion, carrot, celery and garlic, and cook for about 10 minutes or until vegetables soften. Add minced beef and pork, and reduce heat. Fry gently until browned, taking care to break up any lumps. Season with salt and pepper. Pour in wine, and mix well. Simmer, *uncovered*, for a few minutes until wine has almost evaporated.

Add tomatoes and stock, and stir to mix well. Bring to a boil, then reduce heat to low. Leave pan *partly* covered, and simmer very gently for 1½ to 2 hours. Stir occasionally, and add more stock, if necessary.

> **Handy tips**
> **Meat**: beef & pork / veal

Add cream to the sauce, and stir to mix well. Simmer, *uncovered*, for a further 20-30 minutes, stirring frequently.

Cook pasta in a large pan of rapidly boiling salted water until *al dente*, and drain. Serve with meat sauce and a generous sprinkle of grated Parmesan. ***Serves 4***

Spaghetti with Indian-style meat sauce

This is a chunky meat sauce with loads of veggies. It's not 'chilli-hot' (so add 1-2 chillies if you like it really spicy), but there's just a slight kick from the Indian spices, making it refreshingly different!

vegetable oil	500g minced beef
1 medium onion, finely chopped	1 carrot, peeled and grated
2 garlic cloves, finely chopped	1 zucchini, grated
½ tsp fresh ginger, finely chopped	400ml (1 ⅔ cups) tomato passata
½ tsp garam masala	1 tsp dried oregano (optional)
½ tsp ground black pepper	salt (to taste)
¼ tsp ground turmeric	350g to 400g spaghetti (or linguine)
¼ cup tomato paste	

Heat oil over medium-high heat, and fry onion for several minutes until lightly golden. Add garlic and ginger with 1 tablespoon of water, and fry briefly for a minute. Add garam masala, pepper and turmeric, and stir to combine before adding another tablespoon of water. Cook this mixture for another couple of minutes, stirring frequently. Add tomato paste, and stir-fry briefly for a minute. Then add minced beef, and stir to combine thoroughly, taking care to break up any lumps. Cover and simmer over low heat for 20-25 minutes.

> ### *Handy tips*
> **Meat**: beef
>
> **How about** .. serving the meat sauce with basmati rice or even Indian breads

Add carrot, zucchini, tomato passata, oregano (if using), and season with salt. Stir to combine, then cover and cook for another 10-15 minutes.

Cook pasta in a large pan of rapidly boiling salted water until *al dente*, and drain. Serve with meat sauce. ***Serves 3-4***

Quick and Easy Meals

Chinese scrambled eggs with mince

This Chinese recipe of egg and mince is beautifully simple yet absolutely yummy! Soy sauce, wine and sesame oil work wonders with food every time.

300g minced beef, chicken or pork	**1 tsp sugar**
3 tsp sesame oil	**salt and black pepper**
3 tsp light soy sauce (or regular soy)	**8 eggs, beaten**
2 tsp Chinese rice wine or dry sherry (optional)	**¼ cup spring onions, finely chopped**
	2-3 tbsp vegetable oil

Combine minced meat with 2 teaspoons of sesame oil, 2 teaspoons of soy sauce, rice wine, sugar, salt and pepper. Set aside to marinade for 10 minutes or while you're getting the other ingredients ready.

Combine eggs with spring onions, the remaining sesame oil (1 teaspoon) and soy sauce (1 teaspoon). Season with salt and pepper.

In a wok or frying-pan, heat 1 tablespoon of vegetable oil over high heat until it is very hot and slightly smoking. Add minced meat, and stir-fry for a couple of minutes or until browned and *dry*, taking care to break up any lumps. Remove and set aside.

> **Handy tips**
>
> **Meat**: beef / chicken / pork
>
> **How about** .. serving it with steamed rice and stir-fried Asian greens as a main meal

Clean the wok/pan, and heat the remaining vegetable oil (1-2 tablespoons) over high heat. Pour in the egg mixture and allow it to cook, folding and lifting until it begins to set. Return the cooked minced meat to the wok/pan, and stir-fry quickly until the eggs are done. Serve immediately. ***Serves 4***

Vermicelli with meat sauce and green beans

This Chinese stir-fry is a tasty, one-bowl meal and is incredibly versatile - you can put different vegetables in the meat sauce, and instead of rice vermicelli noodles, you can serve it over egg noodles, rice stick noodles or even steamed rice.

350g minced pork, beef or chicken

190g dried rice vermicelli noodles

1 tbsp vegetable oil

1 tbsp fresh garlic, crushed

2 spring onions, finely chopped

200g green beans, sliced diagonally into 3cm lengths

2 tsp corn flour, dissolved in 1 tbsp water

For the marinade:

2 tsp dark soy sauce (or regular soy)

2 tsp Chinese rice wine (or dry sherry)

1 tbsp corn flour

For the sauce:

190ml (¾ cup) chicken stock

2 tbsp oyster sauce

1 tbsp hoisin sauce

1 tbsp sesame oil

2 tsp dark soy sauce (or regular soy)

generous sprinkling of white pepper

For the marinade, combine all ingredients and mix well. Add marinade to minced meat, and stir to combine thoroughly. Allow to stand for 15 minutes or more.

For the sauce, combine all ingredients and mix well.

Cook vermicelli in boiling water for 2 minutes. Drain well and keep warm.

Handy tips

Meat: pork / beef / chicken

In a wok or large frying-pan, heat oil over high heat until it is very hot or slightly smoking. Add garlic and spring onions, and stir-fry very briefly for 30 seconds. Add minced meat, and stir-fry for several minutes or until browned, taking care to break up any lumps. Add beans, and stir-fry for another couple of minutes until softened. Then add the sauce, and bring to a boil. Stir in corn flour/water mixture and cook for another 30 seconds or until sauce boils and thickens.

Divide and place the cooked vermicelli into large serving bowls. Spoon meat sauce on top of each, and serve immediately. ***Serves 2-3***

Stir-fry with broccoli

This fusion-style, stir-fry dish is quick, easy and tasty! If you like it less spicy, add only one chilli, and remove the seeds.

2 tbsp white wine	**3 garlic cloves, crushed**
2 tbsp soy sauce	**1-2 small red chillies, finely chopped**
500g broccoli, cut into florets	**½ x 400g tin chopped tomatoes**
2 tbsp vegetable oil	**salt and black pepper**
500g minced beef, chicken or pork	

Combine wine and soy sauce in a small bowl. Cook broccoli florets by blanching them in boiling water or zapping them in the microwave for 2-3 minutes. Drain and set aside.

In a wok, heat oil over high heat until it is very hot and slightly smoking. Add minced meat, garlic and chillies. Stir-fry for several minutes until meat browns, taking care to break up any lumps.

Add broccoli, and stir-fry for 1-2 minutes or until heated through. Then add tomatoes, and stir to combine. Season with salt and pepper, and stir in wine/soy sauce mixture. Serve with white rice. ***Serves 3-4***

Handy tips

Meat: beef / chicken / pork

How about .. serving it with noodles or even pasta. For a variation, try replacing broccoli with other vegetables such as green beans or zucchinis

Stir-fry with mushrooms

Here's a great Chinese recipe for a delicious but quick and easy meal!

2 tbsp vegetable oil	2 tsp sugar
3 large garlic cloves, finely chopped	250g button mushrooms, sliced
250g minced pork, beef or chicken	1 tbsp Chinese rice wine (or dry sherry)
2 tbsp spring onions, finely chopped	
2 tbsp light soy sauce (or regular soy)	salt and black pepper
3 tbsp water	1 tsp sesame oil

In a wok or large frying-pan, heat half the vegetable oil (1 tablespoon) over high heat until it is very hot and slightly smoking. Add garlic and stir-fry very briefly for 30 seconds. Add minced meat, and stir-fry for a few minutes until browned, taking care to break up any lumps. Add spring onions, soy sauce, water and sugar, and stir-fry for 2-3 minutes. Remove from pan and set aside.

Clean the wok/frying-pan. Add the remaining vegetable oil (1 tablespoon), and heat over high heat until it is very hot. Add mushrooms and stir-fry for about 1 minute. Then add wine, and season with salt and pepper. Stir-fry for several minutes or until mushrooms are cooked, and all the liquid has evaporated.

Return the cooked meat mixture to the wok/pan, and stir-fry for a couple of minutes or until heated through. Remove from heat, and stir in sesame oil. Serve with white rice. ***Serves 2-3***

Handy tips

Meat: pork / beef / chicken

How about .. serving it with noodles or even pasta, for a variation. If you like spicy food, feel free to add 1-2 chillies and fry them with the garlic before adding the minced meat

Stir-fry with chilli and basil

This popular Thai stir-fry is packed with flavours and works well with different types of mince – beef, chicken or pork. I had the opportunity to sample this dish at a Thai restaurant in Sydney recently. It came topped with a crispy fried egg and tasted superb!

2-3 small red chillies, roughly chopped	**500g string beans or green beans, cut into 4-5cm lengths**
6-8 garlic cloves, roughly chopped	**2 tbsp fish sauce**
½ tsp salt flakes/crystals (or regular salt)	**1 tbsp dark soy sauce (or regular soy)**
	2-3 tsp brown (or white) sugar
2 tbsp vegetable oil	**1 cup fresh Thai (or regular) basil leaves, tightly packed**
500g minced beef, chicken or pork	

Combine chillies and garlic with salt, and pound it into a paste using a mortar and pestle. (If you don't have a mortar and pestle, put the chillies and garlic on a chopping board, sprinkle over with salt, and chop finely. Then mash into a coarse paste using the blade of the knife or the back of a spoon.)

> *Handy tips*
>
> **Meat**: beef / chicken / pork

In a wok or large frying-pan, heat oil over high heat until it is very hot and slightly smoking. Add chilli-garlic paste, and stir-fry very briefly for about 30 seconds. Add minced meat, and stir-fry for a few minutes until browned, taking care to break up any lumps. Add beans, and stir-fry for another 4-5 minutes until cooked but not soft.

Combine fish sauce, soy sauce and sugar. Pour into wok/pan, and stir-fry for a further 30 seconds. Remove from heat, and stir in basil leaves. Serve with white rice. ***Serves 4***

Omelettes with pork and bean thread (cha trung)

Egg and mince go well together which is why you find this combination in many Asian cuisines. Here is a recipe that is classic Vietnamese. You can get dried bean thread (also called glass noodles) from Asian grocery stores and some large supermarkets. It's easily confused with rice vermicelli noodles so look out for the words "bean thread" on the packet! Bean thread is much lighter in texture than vermicelli, and is translucent when cooked.

80-100g dried bean thread	¼ tsp black pepper
4-5 dried Chinese (shitake) mushrooms (optional)	½ tsp salt (or to taste)
	vegetable oil (for frying)
250g minced pork	2 tbsp fish sauce (or soy sauce)
8 eggs, beaten	1 small red chilli, finely chopped (optional)
¼ cup spring onions, finely chopped	

In a bowl, cover dried bean thread with warm water, and soak for about 10 minutes or until softened. Rinse under the tap, drain well and cut into 5cm lengths. (If you're using dried Chinese mushrooms, soak these in boiling water for at least 30 minutes. Rinse and squeeze dry. Remove stems, and slice thinly.)

Combine minced pork with eggs, spring onions, black pepper and salt in a bowl. Add bean thread and dried mushrooms (if using). Mix well, taking care to break up any lumps of meat.

Heat a little oil in a non-stick frying-pan over medium heat. Give the egg mixture a good stir, and add about ¼ to the pan. Cook for 3-4 minutes, or until the underside is golden brown. Flip over with a spatula, and cook for another 3 minutes or so until the meat is done and the omelette is golden brown on both sides. Remove from pan and keep warm. Repeat this process with the remaining egg mixture.

Combine fish sauce and chilli (if using) in a small bowl/dish, and serve this on the side with the omelettes.   ***Makes 4***

> **Handy tips**
>
> **Meat**: pork
>
> **How about** .. serving them on crusty baguettes, or with rice and steamed veggies

Egg noodles with satay sauce

This makes a quick and delicious meal that your family will love! Ketjap manis, an Indonesian sweet soy sauce, is widely stocked in Asian food stores and is also available from some supermarkets. If you can't get hold of it, substituting with dark soy sauce (two tablespoons) and sugar (two tablespoons) will also give you a good result.

250g dried egg noodles	**200ml coconut milk**
1 tbsp vegetable oil	**2 tbsp fish sauce**
500g minced pork, beef or chicken	**2 tbsp ketjap manis**
1 onion, roughly chopped	**$1/3$ cup unsalted peanuts, crushed**
1-2 small red chillies, finely chopped (optional)	**2 tbsp fresh coriander, chopped**
2 tbsp good quality satay paste	**lime wedges (to serve)**

Follow instructions on the packet, and cook noodles in rapidly boiling water. Drain well and keep warm.

In a wok, heat oil over high heat until it is very hot and slightly smoking. Add meat and onion. Stir fry for 2-3 minutes or until meat browns. Add chilli (if using) and satay paste, and fry very briefly for about 5 seconds. Add coconut milk, fish sauce, ketjap manis and peanuts. Stir to combine and cook for another 2-3 minutes.

Stir in noodles and coriander, and serve with lime wedges. ***Serves 4***

> ### *Handy tips*
>
> **Meat**: pork / beef / chicken
>
> **How about** .. zapping small florets of broccoli in a microwave for a couple of minutes and tossing them in with the noodles to serve as a one-dish meal

Curry mince with peas (or potatoes)

This dry Indian curry (Kheema) is tasty, quick and low-fuss, and you can easily adjust the spiciness from mild to fiery. There are many recipes for this popular dish – all with slight variations. This version uses peas but if you don't have any peas handy, just replace them with potatoes.

2 tbsp vegetable oil

1 large onion, chopped

1 tsp fresh garlic, crushed

1 tsp fresh ginger, grated

1 tsp garam masala (optional)

1 small red chilli, finely chopped (optional)

500g minced beef, lamb or chicken

2-3 tbsp curry paste or curry powder

200g (1¼ cups) frozen green peas (or 2-3 potatoes, diced)

juice of 1 lemon

salt (to taste)

2 tbsp fresh coriander (or fresh mint), finely chopped

Heat oil in a pan over medium heat. Add onion, garlic, ginger, garam masala (if using) and chilli (if using). Stir-fry for a few minutes or until onion softens. Add mince meat and curry paste. Stir-fry for another few minutes until meat browns, taking care to break up any lumps.

Add peas, lemon juice and season with salt. Reduce heat to low. Cover and simmer for 5 minutes. (If you're not using peas, add potatoes, lemon juice, ¾ cup of hot water and salt. Cover and simmer for 15-25 minutes until potatoes are cooked.)

To finish, stir in coriander, and serve immediately with rice or Indian breads. ***Serves 4***

Handy tips

Meat: beef / lamb / chicken

How about ..
stirring in 2 tbsp yoghurt with the coriander/mint and serving it with a chutney

Russian meat and egg bake

This is a lovely recipe that hails all the way from Russia. It's simple but tasty, and goes well with crusty bread to give you a light but satisfying meal.

20g (1 tbsp) butter	2 tbsp fresh parsley, finely chopped
1 garlic clove, crushed	¼ tsp cinnamon (optional)
1 onion, finely chopped	salt and black pepper
200g lean minced beef or lamb	4 eggs
1 tomato, peeled and chopped	

Preheat oven to 220C (conventional). Heat butter in a pan over medium heat. Fry garlic and onion until onion softens. Add meat and fry until browned, taking care to break up any lumps. Add tomato, parsley, cinnamon (if using), and season with salt and pepper. Turn heat to low, and cook, *uncovered,* for 5-10 minutes or until mixture is *dry*. Stir occasionally to prevent sticking.

Remove meat mixture from heat, and place in a shallow ovenproof dish. Beat eggs with a pinch of salt, and pour over meat. Mix well, and bake in pre-heated oven for 10 minutes or until eggs are set. ***Serves 2***

Handy tips

Meat: beef / lamb

How about .. sprinkling ¼ cup grated Parmesan cheese on top before putting it in the oven. If you don't want to use the oven, simply make 4 holes in the meat mixture in the pan and break an egg into each. Then sprinkle a little paprika on top of the eggs and cover the pan to let it simmer until the eggs are set

Pasta with tomato and sausage sauce

This pasta sauce of sausages, tomatoes and cheese is quick, simple but brilliant. And it's so easy - you can whip it up in less than half an hour. For those who are fond of spicy food, this dish goes particularly well with chillies.

20g (1 tbsp) butter

2-3 garlic cloves, crushed

350g good quality Italian pork sausages, skinned and crumbled

2 x 400g tins whole tomatoes

1-2 small red chillies, chopped (optional)

freshly ground black pepper

350g pasta (rigatoni, spirals or penne)

70g ($^{2}/_{3}$ cup) Parmesan cheese, grated

Heat butter in a pan over medium heat. Add garlic, and fry for about a minute or until golden. Add sausage meat, and fry for several minutes until browned, taking care to break up any lumps. Add tomatoes, chillies (if using) and pepper. Stir to combine and break up the tomatoes. Turn heat to high. Cook, *uncovered,* for about 15 minutes until the sauce is reduced, stirring occasionally.

Cook pasta in a large pan of rapidly boiling salted water until *al dente*. Drain, and toss immediately with sausage sauce and Parmesan. ***Serves 4***

Handy tips

Meat: pork

How about ..
serving it with a green salad

Pasta with wine and sausage sauce

The origin of this dish can be traced to the Emilia-Romagna region in Italy - the home of Parmesan cheese and prosciutto. It's simple but mouth-wateringly good. It uses a fair amount of Parmesan cheese which may explain why it tastes so fantastic!

20g (1 tbsp) butter	1 tbsp tomato paste
1 large onion, finely chopped	freshly ground black pepper
350g good quality Italian pork sausages, skinned and crumbled	350g pasta (spirals, rigatoni or penne)
60ml (¼ cup) white wine	100g (1 cup) Parmesan cheese, grated
60ml (¼ cup) milk	

Heat butter in a pan over medium heat. Add onion, and fry for a few minutes until softened. Add sausage meat, and fry for several minutes until browned, taking care to break up any lumps. Add wine, milk, tomato paste, and pepper, and turn heat to low. Cover and simmer for about 20 minutes.

Cook pasta in a large pan of rapidly boiling salted water until *al dente*. Drain, and toss immediately with sausage sauce and Parmesan. ***Serves 4***

Handy tips

Meat: pork

How about .. serving it with a green salad

Spinach and beef frittata

This is quick and simple to prepare, and is perfect for lunch or a light dinner! You can also serve it as part of a 'spread' if you're entertaining as it is delicious eaten hot or cold.

6 eggs	1 onion, finely chopped
60ml (¼ cup) milk	150g minced beef
1 tbsp Parmesan cheese, grated (optional)	50g (2 large handfuls) spinach leaves
	1 garlic clove, crushed (optional)
2 tbsp extra virgin olive oil	salt and black pepper

Lightly beat eggs with milk in a large bowl. Add Parmesan (if using), and set aside.

In a non-stick frying-pan with a lid to fit, heat 1 tablespoon of oil over medium heat, and fry onion for 2-3 minutes. Add minced beef, and fry until browned, taking care to break up any lumps. Add spinach and garlic (if using), and cook for another minute or until spinach is slightly wilted. Remove from heat, and season with salt and pepper. Add meat/spinach mixture to the beaten eggs, and stir to mix well.

Clean the pan. Heat the remaining oil (1 tablespoon) over low heat, and add the egg mixture to the pan. Cook for 5-8 minutes. Then cover with lid, and cook for another 5-8 minutes or until eggs are set. (If you want a golden brown top, finish cooking under a hot grill instead). *Serves 3-4*

Handy tips

Meat: beef

How about ..
serving it with crusty bread and a green salad. For variation, try replacing the spinach with 1-2 tbsp flat-leaf parsley, rocket or a mixture of fresh herbs

Chilli con carne

If you don't have a favourite recipe for this popular Mexican dish, here is a simple one that is easy to prepare and cooks in no time.

olive oil	2 tbsp tomato paste
1 large onion, finely chopped	2 tsp chilli powder (or to taste)
2 garlic cloves, crushed	1 tsp dried oregano
500g minced beef	1 x 400g tin red kidney beans, rinsed and drained
1 x 400g tin chopped tomatoes	
125ml (½ cup) beef stock	salt (to taste)
1 tbsp cocoa powder	

Heat a little oil in a large frying-pan over medium heat. Add onion and garlic, and fry for a few minutes until onion softens. Turn heat to high, and add minced beef. Fry for several minutes until browned, taking care to break up any lumps. Add tomatoes, stock, cocoa powder, tomato paste, chilli powder and oregano. Turn heat to low, and simmer, *uncovered,* for 15 minutes.

Add beans and season with salt. Simmer for a few more minutes, or until beans are heated through. Serve with corn chips/tacos as a starter, or tortillas/burritos as a main meal.
Serves 6 as a starter; Serves 4 as a main meal

Handy tips

Meat: beef

How about ..
serving it with guacamole, chopped fresh tomatoes, grated cheese and/or sour cream

Classic American burgers

The hamburger easily ranks as one of the world's most popular dishes, and volumes have been published on it. So what makes a great hamburger? A dominant view is to use good, fresh meat (and plenty of it), with the bun being regarded at best a 'sideshow', and at worst a 'distraction'. Minced sirloin, round and chuck steak are the recommended cuts, but these shouldn't be too lean as a 10%-20% fat content is often held as the ideal. This recipe uses butter but feel free to replace it with extra virgin olive oil.

For the burgers:

4 slices (1cm thick) red onion (optional)

30g (1½ tbsp) butter, melted

salt and freshly ground black pepper

700g sirloin, round or chuck steak, minced

4 hamburger buns

For the toppings (choice of any or all):

lettuce leaves

ripe tomatoes, sliced

bacon, cooked

dill pickles, sliced (or sweet pickles)

tomato sauce, mustard and mayonnaise

Preheat grill or barbecue to high. (If using onion slices, brush them on both sides with melted butter, and season with salt and pepper. Place them on the grill/barbecue, and cook for 4 minutes each side. Remove from heat, and set aside.)

Shape minced beef into 4 round patties. Brush one side of the patties with melted butter, and season with salt and black pepper. Cook patties on grill or barbecue, buttered side first. Turn over *once*, and cook on the other side until cooked through, brushing them with butter, and seasoning well.

When the patties are almost done, cut the buns into halves, and brush the cut sides of the buns with the remaining butter. Toast for about 2 minutes.

Place patties, toppings and onion slices (if using) on buns. Serve immediately. ***Serves 4***

Handy tips

Meat: beef

How about ..
making them into cheeseburgers. About 2-3 minutes before the patties are done, place a slice of Cheddar or Swiss cheese on top of each patty and cook until the cheese melts

Meatloaves and Terrines

Meatloaf with Italian sausages and eggs

This meatloaf is beautifully flavoured with fresh herbs, and the hard-boiled eggs in the middle just give it a fantastic visual presentation!

800g lean minced beef	**1 tbsp fresh oregano, chopped**
250g good quality Italian pork sausages, skinned and crumbled	**50g (½ cup) Parmesan cheese, grated**
1 medium red onion, finely chopped	**½ tsp salt (or to taste)**
2 tbsp flat-leaf parsley, finely chopped	**1 tsp freshly ground black pepper**
1 tbsp fresh thyme	**1 large egg, separated**
	3 hard-boiled eggs, shelled

Preheat oven to 180C (conventional). Line a baking tray with foil, leaving enough at both ends to seal in the meatloaf later. Grease foil with a little olive oil.

In a large bowl, combine minced beef with sausage meat using your hands. Make a hole in the centre of the mixture with your fist, and add onion, parsley, thyme, oregano, and Parmesan. Season with salt and pepper. Mix to combine thoroughly. Make a hole again in the centre of the mixture. Add egg yolk and mix well. (If you wish to check seasoning, fry a small lump of meat mixture – taste and adjust.)

Divide meat mixture into 2 halves. Shape one half into a log of about 5cm x 20cm. Place the hard-boiled eggs, end to end, down the middle, and press them gently into the meat. Make

> **Handy tips**
> **Meat**: beef & pork

another log of the same size with the remaining half of the meat mixture, and put it on top of the first log. Mould the 2 logs carefully into one – make sure you mould the mixture gently around the eggs to keep them centred. Place meatloaf onto the lined baking tray. Then beat egg white lightly, and brush it over the top and sides. Finally, bring the two long ends of the foil over the top of the meatloaf, and crimp the edges to seal and cover the meatloaf completely.

Bake in pre-heated oven for 40 minutes. Remove from oven and open the foil (careful you don't get burned by the escaping steam!) Return meatloaf to oven, and bake, *uncovered,* for another 30 minutes or until browned and cooked through. (If necessary, test by piercing meatloaf with a skewer – any liquid running out should be clear.) Remove from oven, and allow to stand for 5-10 minutes before serving. ***Serves 6***

Meatloaf with wine, tomatoes and mushrooms

In this gorgeous Italian recipe, the meatloaf is first browned and then baked slowly in a wine sauce. It's beautifully moist and succulent, and is delicious as leftover the next day.

100g pancetta (or bacon), finely chopped	freshly ground black pepper
	dry breadcrumbs (for coating)
1 large bread roll (white or wholemeal)	150g brown (or button) mushrooms, chopped
1 kg lean minced veal or beef (or ½ veal, ½ beef)	4 tbsp olive oil
150g Parmesan cheese, grated	160mls (⅔ cup) white or red wine
1 large onion, finely chopped	4-5 tomatoes, peeled and chopped
2 garlic cloves, finely chopped	2 small pieces of lemon peel (1 x 2cm), finely sliced
2 eggs	
½ tsp salt (or to taste)	

Fry pancetta until it begins to crisp, and reserve fat for later use. In a bowl, cover bread roll with water, and leave to soak for 10-15 minutes. Squeeze away excess water, and combine with pancetta, minced meat, Parmesan, onion, garlic and eggs. Season with salt and pepper, and mix well with your hands. (If you wish to check seasoning, fry a small lump of meat mixture – taste and adjust.) Shape meat mixture into a loaf, and pack firmly. Refrigerate for 1 hour or more. (This helps the meatloaf to stay together when you're browning it later.)

Preheat oven to 160C (conventional). Coat meatloaf all over with breadcrumbs. In a non-stick, frying-pan over medium heat, fry the mushrooms in 1 tablespoon of oil. Remove from pan, and set aside. Clean the pan.

> **Handy tips**
>
> **Meat**: veal / beef
>
> **How about** .. serving it with boiled new potatoes and a salad of greens

Heat the remaining oil (3 tablespoons) together with the pancetta fat. Gently ease meatloaf into the pan and brown it on the bottom. Turn over carefully, and brown it on top – you may find it easier to do this with 2 spatulas. (If you're not worried about the meatloaf breaking, try and brown it on 4 sides.) Remove meatloaf and place in a baking dish, again using 2 spatulas to make it easier. Tip excess oil from the pan, and add the fried mushrooms, wine, tomatoes and lemon peel. Bring to a boil, and pour into baking dish with the meatloaf.

Bake in pre-heated oven for about 2 hours or until cooked through. (If necessary, test by piercing meatloaf with a skewer – any liquid running out should be clear.) If liquid in the baking dish is drying out, add more wine. If there is too much liquid when it is cooked, reduce liquid in a saucepan, and serve with meatloaf. Allow meatloaf to stand for 5-10 minutes before serving. ***Serves 6***

Meatloaf with mushroom sauce

This recipe is American-Italian - the addition of cracker crumbs and milk gives the meatloaf a light texture, and a sauce flavoured with the rich, earthy tone of Porcini mushrooms nicely complements it. To make two-thirds of a cup of crumbs, you'd need slightly less than a 250g packet of plain cracker biscuits. If you don't have a food processor or grinder, simply replace the cracker crumbs with ½ cup of good quality dry breadcrumbs from bakeries or gourmet grocery stores.

1 tbsp olive oil

1 medium red onion, finely chopped

3 garlic cloves, crushed

250ml (1 cup) milk

1 tsp fresh thyme

2 tbsp Dijon mustard

1 tbsp Worcestershire sauce

½ tsp Tabasco sauce

2 eggs, lightly beaten

900g minced meat (equal parts of beef, pork and veal)

²/₃ cup cracker biscuit crumbs

¼ cup flat-leaf parsley, finely chopped

½ tsp salt (or to taste)

½ tsp freshly ground black pepper

For the mushroom sauce:

15g dried porcini mushrooms

40g (2 tbsp) unsalted butter

2 garlic cloves, crushed

100g field (or brown-gilled) mushrooms, diced

375ml (1½ cups) beef stock

1 tbsp plain flour, dissolved in 4 tbsp water

Preheat oven to 180C (conventional), and line a baking tray with baking paper. Heat oil in a frying-pan over medium heat. Add onion and garlic, and fry for several minutes until onion softens. Remove from heat, and set aside to cool.

In a large bowl, add milk, thyme, mustard, Worcestershire sauce, Tabasco sauce and eggs. Stir to mix well. Add the onion/garlic mixture, minced meat, biscuit crumbs and parsley. Season with salt and pepper, and combine well using your hands. (If you wish to check seasoning, fry a small lump of meat mixture – taste and adjust.) Place meat mixture onto the lined baking tray, and shape into a

Handy tips

Meat: beef, pork & veal

How about .. serving it with mashed potatoes and salad or buttered vegies

loaf. Bake in pre-heated oven for 1 hour or until cooked through. (If necessary, test by piercing meatloaf with a skewer – any liquid running out should be clear.)

To make the mushroom sauce, grind the porcini mushrooms in a spice/coffee grinder. Heat half the butter (1 tablespoon) in a pan over medium heat, and fry garlic and field mushrooms until softened. Remove from pan and set aside. Add stock to the pan you have used to fry the mushrooms, and bring to a boil. Cook for about 10 minutes or until stock is reduced by about one-quarter. Remove from heat and stir in ground porcini. Add the garlic/mushroom mixture and the flour/water mixture to the porcini stock. Return to heat, and simmer gently until the sauce thickens, stirring frequently. Before removing from heat, stir in the remaining butter (1 tablespoon).

Allow meatloaf to stand for 5-10 minutes once it is removed from the oven. Serve with mushroom sauce on the side. ***Serves 6-8***

Meatloaf wrapped in shortcrust pastry

This gorgeous dish is from Scandinavia. Wrapped in homemade, shortcrust pastry, the meatloaf tastes fantastic and looks impressive! If you don't have the means to crumb bread, simply use three tablespoons of dry breadcrumbs that are sold in some bakeries and specialty grocers.

For the shortcrust pastry:

200g butter

300g (2 cups) plain flour

60ml (¼ cup) ice-cold water

extra flour (for rolling out pastry)

For the meatloaf:

1 small onion, finely chopped

1 rasher bacon, finely chopped

knob of butter

1 slice sandwich bread (white or wholemeal), crumbed

100ml (5 tbsp) pouring cream

100ml (5 tbsp) white wine

400g minced beef, veal or pork

½ tsp salt (or to taste)

½ tsp white pepper

To make the pastry, cut the butter up into thin 5cm pieces, and pulse them together with flour and water in a food processor until the mixture resembles breadcrumbs. (If you don't have a food processor, soften the butter. Then mix it with the other ingredients using your hands or a hand-held

> **Handy tips**
> **Meat**: beef / veal / pork

beater with fittings for dough.) Bring this crumbly mixture together into a dough with your hands. Don't over-work it or the pastry will turn hard and heavy. Wrap in cling wrap, and refrigerate for 1 hour.

Preheat oven to 220C (conventional), and grease a baking tray. Fry onion and bacon in butter until onion softens and bacon starts to crisp. Set aside to cool. Mix breadcrumbs with cream and wine, and allow to stand for about 10 minutes. Combine breadcrumb mixture with onion/bacon mixture, minced meat, salt and pepper. (If you wish to check seasoning, fry a small lump of meat mixture – taste and adjust.) Shape the meat mixture into a loaf on a piece of moistened baking paper.

Sprinkle pastry very lightly with flour and place between 2 pieces of cling wrap. Roll out pastry so that it is big enough to wrap around the meatloaf. Gently ease the meatloaf onto the pastry. Fold up the pastry at the short ends, and trim away excess pastry at the corners, (reserving this for decoration, if it takes your fancy).

Then fold up the long sides. (Don't do this too tightly!) Press and smooth to seal the joints, and trim excess pastry. Gently move the wrapped-up meatloaf onto a greased baking tray, (and decorate with trimmings if you want). Bake in pre-heated oven for 40-45 minutes. ***Serves 4-6***

Country-style meatloaf with tomato topping

This will go down well with kids as it is topped with tomatoes cooked in brown sugar. When you invert the meatloaf, resist the temptation to throw away the juice from the meat. Pan-fry some broccoli (or other veggies) with chopped garlic, pour over the meat juice, cook for a few minutes and serve it with the meatloaf. Yum!

For the tomato topping:

1 small red onion, finely chopped

1 tbsp olive oil

1 tomato, roughly chopped

½ cup brown sugar

For the meatloaf:

1 kg minced beef

¾ cup dry breadcrumbs

1 onion, finely chopped

2 carrots, peeled and grated

2 zucchinis, grated

2 eggs

2 tbsp fresh parsley, finely chopped

1 tsp fresh rosemary, chopped

2 tbsp Worcestershire sauce

1 tsp ground nutmeg

¾ tsp salt (or to taste)

black pepper

To make the tomato topping, fry onion in oil until softened. Add tomato and sugar. Cook until mixture thickens, and set aside.

Preheat oven to 180C (conventional), and line a loaf tin with baking paper. Combine all ingredients for the meatloaf and mix well. (If you wish to check seasoning, fry a small lump of meat mixture – taste and adjust.) Place meat mixture in the lined loaf tin, and bake in pre-heated oven for 45 minutes.

> **Handy tips**
>
> **Meat**: beef
>
> **How about** .. serving it with mash and broccoli fried in a little meat juice. (If you wish, you could also make a gravy from the meat juice).

Remove meatloaf from oven, and turn it upside down onto a baking tray (saving the juice if you wish). Return meatloaf to the oven and bake for another 20 minutes.
Then remove meatloaf from oven again, and spread tomato topping on top. Then finish off with another 10 minutes in the oven. ***Serves 6-8***

Chicken and pork terrine with pistachios

This is simple to prepare and great for summer lunches! It's made a day ahead and frees you to attend to other things if you're entertaining.

25-28 thin rashers pancetta (or rindless bacon)	50g (¹/₃ cup) dried cranberries (optional)
1 tbsp extra virgin olive oil	2 garlic cloves, crushed
1 onion, finely chopped	1 heaped tbsp flat leaf parsley, chopped
500g minced chicken	
500g minced pork	1 heaped tbsp fresh thyme
100ml (5 tbsp) brandy (or dry sherry)	2 eggs, lightly beaten
75g (½ cup) pistachio nut kernels, cut into halves	1 tsp salt (or to taste)
	freshly ground black pepper

Preheat oven to 180C (conventional), and lightly grease a loaf tin. Line the base and sides with pancetta slices, allowing them to overlap slightly but leaving enough to cover the top later.

Heat a little oil in a pan, and fry onion until soft (but not browned). Allow to cool, and combine with all remaining ingredients, mixing thoroughly using your hands. (If you wish to check seasoning, fry a small lump of meat mixture – taste and adjust.) Pack the meat mixture tightly into the tin, and cover with the remaining pancetta slices. Then cover and seal the top of the tin with foil.

Handy tips

Meat: chicken & pork

Fill a deep baking tray with boiling water about half way up the terrine tin. Bake the terrine in this water bath in the pre-heated oven for 1¼ hours or until firm to the touch. Remove terrine from tin, and allow to cool. Trim a piece of cardboard to fit on top of the terrine, and place a heavy weight on it (e.g. some cans or a foil-covered brick). Refrigerate overnight. *Serves 6-8*

Pork and veal terrine with rum and cream

This terrine is made two days ahead to allow ample time for the flavours to develop. It's really easy to prepare and a great starter if you're entertaining.

500g minced pork	4 eschalots, finely chopped
500g minced veal	2 tsp fresh thyme
100ml (5 tbsp) white wine	15 peppercorns, crushed
60ml (¼ cup) rum	12 juniper berries, lightly crushed
100ml thick (or double) cream	1¼ tsp salt (or to taste)
2 eggs, lightly beaten	2 bay leaves
4 garlic cloves, crushed	

Preheat oven to 180C (conventional), and lightly grease a loaf tin.

Combine all ingredients (except bay leaves), and mix thoroughly using your hands. (If you wish to check seasoning, fry a small lump of meat mixture – taste and adjust). Pack the meat mixture tightly into the tin, and place the bay leaves on top. Then cover and seal the top of the tin with foil.

> **Handy tips**
> **Meat**: pork & veal

Fill a deep baking tray with boiling water about half way up the tin. Bake the terrine in this water bath in the pre-heated oven for 1½ hours or until firm to the touch. Remove from tin, and allow to cool. Refrigerate for 48 hours before serving. ***Serves 6-8***

Other Starters and Main Meals

Asia

Japanese beef and pumpkin stew

Quick, easy and healthy without any compromise on taste – that's the only way to describe this dish from Japan. It uses a fair amount of fresh ginger which makes it particularly tempting to those of us who are fans of this spicy root. The pumpkin is meant to stay reasonably whole so don't overcook it or it will turn to mush. Feel free to vary the quantities of beef used depending on your taste preference and what you have in stock.

2 tbsp fresh ginger, grated	400g minced beef
2 tbsp sake (or white wine)	500g butternut pumpkin, peeled, seeded and cubed (3-5cm)
4 tbsp Japanese soy sauce (or regular soy)	2 tsp corn flour, dissolved in 1 tbsp water
3 tbsp sugar	

In a pan, combine 1 tablespoon of ginger, 1 tablespoon of sake, 3 tablespoons of soy sauce and 2 tablespoons of sugar, and bring to a boil. Add minced beef and cook for 4-5 minutes, stirring to break up any lumps.

Add pumpkin with the remaining sake (1 tablespoon), soy sauce (1 tablespoon) and sugar (1 tablespoon) to the pan. Then add enough water to cover about half of the pumpkin. Bring to a boil before reducing heat to low. Cover and simmer for 15-20 minutes or until pumpkin is cooked (but not mushy). Stir gently from time to time to turn over pumpkin cubes so that they are cooked evenly.

Handy tips
Meat: beef

Using a slatted spoon, transfer pumpkin to a serving dish, and keep warm, if possible. Add corn flour mixture to the beefy broth in the pan, and stir to mix well. Allow it to bubble for a few minutes, *uncovered*, until sauce thickens. Pour over pumpkin, garnish with the remaining ginger (1 tablespoon), and serve with steamy white rice. ***Serves 3-4***

Korean meatballs

These meatballs are an absolute delight, and they have a beautiful aroma from the toasted sesame seeds! The Koreans usually serve them as one of many side dishes. But if you're not doing this, why not serve them as a 'wrap-your-own' with steamed rice and lettuce leaves? Simply put a meatball and a spoonful of rice in a lettuce leaf, wrap it up and enjoy! It's a meal-in-one, and a bit of fun for the kids.

2½ tbsp sesame seeds	2 tsp sesame oil
½ tsp salt flakes/crystals (or regular salt)	1 tsp sugar
	¼ tsp black pepper
500g lean minced beef	plain flour (for coating)
4 spring onions, finely chopped	2 eggs, lightly beaten
4 garlic cloves, crushed	vegetable oil (for frying)
1-2 tbsp Japanese soy sauce (or regular soy)	

Lightly toast sesame seeds under a grill on low heat. (Keep a watchful eye while you're doing this because sesame seeds burn really easily.) Grind them with salt using a mortar and pestle or a spice/meat grinder.

Combine the crushed sesame seeds with minced beef, spring onions, garlic, soy sauce, sesame oil, sugar and pepper. Mix well using your hands. (If you wish to check seasoning, fry a small lump of meat mixture – taste and adjust.) Cover and refrigerate for at least 30 minutes, and shape into flat meatballs or rissoles.

> **Handy tips**
> **Meat**: beef

Coat meatballs/rissoles lightly in flour. Dip them in eggs and drain off excess. (It's better to shape all the meatballs first *before* coating them in flour and eggs or your hands will get really sticky.)

In a non-stick frying-pan, heat a little oil, and fry meatballs/rissoles for 4-6 minutes each side or until cooked through. ***Serves 3-4***

Sang choi bao

I've chosen this recipe because it makes a light and 'healthy' dish that's full of crunch - you'd feel as though you're biting into freshness itself! To remove lettuce leaves without tearing, place whole lettuce on kitchen bench with its core/stem facing down. Then give it a few whacks in a downward movement using the palm of your hand. To julienne a carrot, run a vegetable peeler down its length to make thin strips before cutting the strips into a fine julienne.

2 tbsp vegetable oil	**1 tsp sugar**
200g minced pork, chicken or beef	**1 tsp oyster sauce**
1 large garlic clove, finely chopped	**¼ tsp sesame oil**
1 tbsp fresh ginger, julienned	**1 small carrot, julienned**
½ small red onion, finely chopped	**1 celery stalk, finely chopped**
3 button mushrooms, stems removed and sliced	**¼ cup spring onions, finely chopped**
	4 iceberg lettuce leaves, washed and dried
1 tbsp Chinese rice wine (or dry sherry)	
1 tbsp light soy sauce (or regular soy)	**handful of fresh coriander (for garnish – optional)**

Heat vegetable oil in a wok or large frying-pan over high heat until it is very hot and slightly smoking. Add minced meat, garlic and ginger, and stir-fry for 1-2 minutes, taking care to break up any lumps. Add onion and mushrooms, and stir-fry very briefly for about 30 seconds.

Next add wine, soy sauce, sugar, oyster sauce and sesame oil. Stir-fry for another minute or until the meat is cooked through. Add carrot, celery and spring onions. Stir to mix well, and remove from heat.

Place the lettuce leaves on serving plates. Spoon meat mixture onto the leaves, and garnish with coriander (if using). ***Serves 2-4 as a starter***

> ### Handy tips
>
> **Meat**: pork / chicken / beef
>
> **How about** .. serving it with white rice as a main meal for two. For variation, toss in ½ cup fresh bean sprouts together with the carrot and celery

Mongolian beef

This recipe is refreshingly different from the oily fare that's dished up in some Chinese restaurants! It makes no compromise on taste, yet it's 'light' and big on crunch and freshness.

500g lean minced beef

4 cups Chinese cabbage (less than ½ a cabbage), finely shredded

2 tsp salt flakes (or regular salt)

2-3 tbsp vegetable oil

2 tbsp Chinese rice wine (or dry sherry)

2 tbsp hoisin sauce

1 tbsp oyster sauce

1 tsp malt vinegar

½ tsp sesame oil

1 small carrot, finely chopped

½ red capsicum, finely sliced

½ cup spring onions, finely sliced

For the marinade:

2 large garlic cloves, crushed

1 tsp fresh ginger, grated

1 tbsp corn flour

1 tbsp light soy sauce (or regular soy)

1 tbsp Chinese rice wine (or dry sherry)

¼ tsp sesame oil

Combine minced beef with all the ingredients for the marinade. Cover and refrigerate for 30 minutes or more.

Using your hands, mix cabbage well with salt, and allow to stand for 15 minutes. Rinse under a cold tap, and drain. Squeeze away excess liquid.

> **Handy tips**
> **Meat**: beef

In a wok or large frying-pan, heat oil over high heat until it is very hot and slightly smoking. Add half of the minced beef, and stir-fry very briefly for 30 seconds, taking care to break up any lumps. Remove from wok and set aside. Then add more oil to the wok, and stir-fry the remaining half of the meat. Return all the cooked beef to the wok, and add wine, hoisin sauce, oyster sauce, vinegar and sesame oil. Stir-fry very briefly for 30 seconds.

Finish by adding the cabbage, carrot and capsicum, and stir fry for a minute or two. Toss in spring onions, mix well and serve with white rice. ***Serves 3-4***

Chinese meatballs with lettuce

This recipe is inspired by the dish, "Lion's Head" which are huge meatballs served on New Year's Day in the bygone era. There is a recipe for this dish in almost every Chinese cookbook - the one below is an amalgamation of several recipe ideas with one significant departure from the traditional. Instead of making huge meatballs (each weighing 80g-120g) which have to be stewed for hours, I've made much smaller ones so that they can be cooked and shared around more easily. As they sit beautifully on a bed of lettuce, all you do is to serve them with steamed rice, and you'll have a delicious meal for your family!

250ml (1 cup) chicken stock	**1 tbsp light soy sauce (or regular soy)**
2 tbsp Chinese rice wine (or dry sherry)	**1 tbsp Chinese rice wine (or dry sherry)**
2 tsp light soy sauce (or regular soy)	**600g minced pork**
1 iceberg lettuce, leaves separated and washed	**3 tbsp spring onions, finely chopped**
salt (to taste)	**1 tsp fresh ginger, grated**
	2 tsp brown (or white) sugar
1 tsp corn flour, dissolved in 2 tsp water	**1 egg white**
	¼ tsp salt (or to taste)
For the meatballs:	**vegetable oil (for frying)**
1 tbsp corn flour	

To make the meatballs, mix corn flour with soy sauce and rice wine. Combine with all other ingredients for meatballs (except oil), and mix well using your hands. Shape heaped tablespoons of meat mixture into balls.

In a pan (preferably non-stick) with a lid to fit, heat oil over medium heat, and quickly fry meatballs until lightly browned all over. Do not crowd the pan – fry in batches, if necessary. Tip away all but 1 tablespoon of oil from the pan.

Handy tips
Meat: pork

Return all meatballs to the pan and add stock, wine and soy sauce. Bring sauce to a simmering point. Cover and simmer over low heat for 20-25 minutes, turning meatballs over occasionally to coat them evenly with sauce.

Just before the meatballs are ready, bring a large pan of water to the boil. Blanch lettuce leaves very briefly for about 30 seconds or until slightly softened. Drain well and place on a large serving plate.

Remove meatballs from pan, and arrange them on top of the lettuce. Adjust seasoning of the sauce left in the pan, if necessary. Give the corn flour/water mixture a good stir, and add it gradually into the sauce, stirring constantly. Stir and cook for another minute or until sauce thickens slightly. Pour sauce on top of the meatballs and lettuce. Serve immediately with steamed rice.
Serves 3-4

Cantonese steamed pork

Steamed pork has long been popular with home cooks in Hong Kong - it is delicious and yet easy to prepare. This recipe is a modern treatment of this old favourite (my niece first put me onto it, and she raved about it!) The large amount of water added to the pork gives it a tender, melt-in-your-mouth feel. It may seem a little unusual but try it, and you'll be delighted with the result!

400g lean minced pork	**1 tsp sesame oil**
60ml (¼ cup) light soy sauce (or regular soy)	**½ tsp Chinese rice wine or dry sherry (optional)**
2 tsp corn flour	**2 tsp vegetable oil**
1 tsp sugar	**250ml (1 cup) water**

In a bowl or a dish, combine minced pork with all ingredients (except water). Mix well.

Add water *gradually* to the pork, stirring and mixing as the water is added. (You should end up with so much water in the pork that you won't be able to pick it up in one big piece).

Place bowl/dish in a steamer, and steam for 20-30 minutes or until the pork is cooked through. (If you don't have a steamer, place a rack in a deep pan with about 4 cm of boiling water at the bottom. Lower the bowl/dish onto the rack. Then cover, and steam until the meat is done.) There will be a fair amount of broth in the bowl. Don't worry – serve it with rice, and the broth will go really well with it! ***Serves 2-3***

Handy tips

Meat: pork

How about .. serving it with fried veggies Asian-style. Heat oil in a wok/frying-pan, and fry 3-4 finely chopped garlic cloves for about 30 seconds. Add 500-600g snow peas/broccoli, ½ tsp salt, ¼ tsp sugar (optional), and ¼ cup chicken stock. Stir to mix well. Then cover, and cook for about 4-5 minutes or until veggies are cooked to your taste

Steamed dumplings

These Chinese dumplings (or Jiao Zi) are quickly blanched and then served with a dark, piquant sauce of soy and vinegar. A touch of chilli adds zing – you can get chilli oil from Asian grocery stores where you can also get wonton wrappers and Chinese red rice vinegar. They are fabulous as starters for dinner parties.

30 (1 packet) wonton wrappers

For the sauce:

2 tsp Asian shallot (or eschallot), grated

2 tsp garlic, crushed

1½ tbsp dark soy sauce (or regular soy)

¾ tsp sugar

3 tsp Chinese red rice vinegar (or red wine vinegar)

2 tsp sesame oil

2-3 tbsp chilli oil (optional)

For the filling:

300g minced pork

3 garlic cloves, crushed

¾ tsp salt (or to taste)

generous sprinkling of white pepper

To make the sauce, combine all ingredients in a bowl, and set aside.

To make the filling, combine all ingredients and mix well. Take a wonton wrapper and brush the edges with a little water. Put a teaspoon of meat mixture in the centre of the wrapper, and fold it into a triangle. Take 2 corners of the triangle, and fold them over each other, and pinch. Repeat this process for all remaining wrappers and filling.

> **Handy tips**
> **Meat**: pork

Bring a large pot of water to the boil. Drop wontons gently into the boiling water. Reduce heat, and simmer for about 3 minutes or until meat is cooked through. Remove wontons with a slotted spoon. Drain, and serve with sauce on the side, or poured on top. ***Serves 4-5 as a starter***

Fried rice with beef and lettuce

You can find this dish in almost every Chinese restaurant, and many Chinese home cooks are armed with their own version of this recipe. This is my version which has served me well on many occasions! The secret to good fried rice is to fry it over high heat, and to ensure the key ingredients are dry. Day-old rice is the best, but if you can't plan ahead, cook the rice at least two hours beforehand. Then cool and refrigerate until ready for use as it helps to remove moisture from the freshly-cooked rice.

300g minced beef	**2-3 large garlic cloves, finely chopped**
2 tbsp light soy sauce (or regular soy)	**¼ cup spring onions, finely sliced**
generous sprinklings of white pepper	**6 cups long grain rice, cooked at least 2 hours before (see above comments)**
4 tbsp vegetable oil	
3 or 4 eggs, lightly beaten	**2 cups iceberg lettuce, shredded**
salt (to taste)	

Marinade minced beef with half of the soy sauce (1 tablespoon) and a generous sprinkling of white pepper, and let it stand for 10 minutes or more. Heat 1 tablespoon of oil in a pan, and stir-fry meat until browned and *dry*, taking care to break up any lumps. Remove from pan, and set aside. Clean the pan.

Season eggs with salt. Heat another tablespoon of oil, and fry the eggs into an omelette. Just before it sets completely, break the omelette up into small pieces with the spatula. Remove from pan and set aside.

> **Handy tips**
>
> **Meat**: beef
>
> **How about** .. serving it with chilli sauce and soy sauce on the side

In a wok, heat the remaining oil (2 tablespoons) over high heat until it is very hot and slightly smoking. Add garlic, spring onions, salt, and another generous sprinkling of pepper. Stir-fry briefly for 30 seconds. Add rice and stir constantly, taking care to break up any lumps and to prevent it from sticking. When the rice is heated through (after several minutes), add lettuce and the remaining soy sauce (1 tablespoon). Stir-fry for another minute or until lettuce softens a little. Then add the cooked beef and eggs to the wok. Stir to combine well, and serve immediately. ***Serves 4***

Spicy fried rice

The secret to making good Asian fried rice is to fry it over high heat and to ensure the key ingredients are dry. Day-old rice is the best, but if you can't plan ahead, cook the rice at least two hours beforehand. Then cool and refrigerate until ready for use as it helps to remove moisture from the freshly-cooked rice.

3 tbsp vegetable oil	6 cups long grain rice, cooked at least 2 hours before (see above comments)
400g minced beef or chicken	3 spring onions, finely sliced
3-4 garlic cloves, finely chopped	75g (½ cup) frozen green peas, cooked and drained
2 tsp fresh ginger, finely chopped	
1 tbsp curry powder/paste	1 tsp salt (or to taste)

Heat 1 tablespoon of oil in a wok, and stir-fry minced meat until browned and *dry*, taking care to break up any lumps. Remove from wok, and set aside. Clean the wok.

Heat the remaining oil (2 tablespoons) over high heat until it is very hot and slightly smoking. Add garlic, ginger and curry powder/paste, and stir-fry very briefly for about 30 seconds. Return the cooked meat to the wok, and add rice, spring onions, peas and salt. Stir-fry for about 4-5 minutes or until rice is heated through. Serve immediately. ***Serves 4***

> **Handy tips**
>
> **Meat**: beef / chicken
>
> **How about** .. adding 1-2 chopped chillies to the curry powder/paste if you like it spicy

Beef rice porridge (congee)

The Chinese call this "jook", and every Chinese home-cook has a recipe of his/her own. This is my recipe which I've used on many Sunday evenings after long lunches. It's filling and satisfying without being too heavy, and while it may take a little while to cook, it is really quite easy to prepare. The egg gives the congee a lovely creaminess - it is by no means a critical ingredient and can be left out altogether. Make sure you use a big or deep pot for the congee as it bubbles over easily.

500g minced beef	½ tsp salt
2 tbsp soy sauce	1 tbsp vegetable oil (optional)
¼ tsp sugar	4 eggs (optional)
salt and white pepper	1-2 spring onions, finely chopped
1 cup white rice (preferably short grain)	extra white pepper and soy sauce (to serve)
2 litres (8 cups) water	

Combine minced beef with soy sauce and sugar. Season with salt and pepper, and mix well. Cover and refrigerate for 30 minutes or more. Shape meat mixture into small balls.

Place rice and water in a deep/big pot, and bring to a boil. Stir to loosen rice grains from the bottom of the pot. Reduce heat to low. Cover and simmer gently for 1 to 1½ hours, stirring occasionally to prevent from sticking to the bottom. (The congee is ready when it acquires a thick, gruel-like consistency.)

When the congee is ready, turn heat to medium-low. Add salt and oil (if using), and drop meatballs gently into the congee. Cover and cook for a few minutes or until the meatballs are done.

> **Handy tips**
>
> **Meat**: beef
>
> **How about** .. adding thin strips of ginger to the spring onion before ladling the congee into the bowls. You can also cook the congee in stock (or half stock, half water)

In each of 4 pasta-sized bowls, crack an egg (if using), and add a sprinkling of spring onion. Ladle the piping hot congee into the bowls. Stir immediately with a spoon to mix the raw egg well with the congee. Serve with a sprinkle of white pepper, and extra soy sauce on the side. *Serves 4*

Macanese meatballs

These meatballs from the cuisine of Macau are easy to make and taste terrific with the mint really working its magic! They're great as finger food (just stick a toothpick in each for easy handling), but you can also serve them as a main meal with steamed rice and Asian greens.

500g minced beef

¼ cup fresh mint leaves, finely chopped

2 spring onions, finely chopped

2 garlic cloves, crushed

2 tbsp light soy sauce (or regular soy)

1 tsp corn flour

1 egg white

salt and white pepper

vegetable oil (for grilling/frying)

Combine all ingredients (except oil), and mix well using your hands. (If you wish to check seasoning, fry a small lump of meat mixture – taste and adjust.) Cover and refrigerate for 30 minutes or more. Shape into flat meatballs or patties/rissoles.

Brush with oil and grill/barbecue or pan-fry. ***Serves 5-6 as a starter; Serves 3-4 as a main meal***

> **Handy tips**
>
> **Meat**: beef

Filipino picadillo

Picadillo is a dish that can be found in many countries that have come under the Spanish influence (e.g. Mexico, Cuba and Latin America). I'm told that the name comes from the Spanish word "picar" which means "to mince or chop". This is a Filipino version of picadillo, and is a brothy stew of minced beef and vegetables. It makes a tasty family meal, and goes particularly well with rice.

500g minced beef	**1 carrot, chopped**
1 tbsp fish sauce (or regular soy)	**2 potatoes, cubed**
¾ tsp ground black pepper	**500ml (2 cups) beef stock (or ½ stock, ½ water)**
1-2 tbsp vegetable oil	
4-5 garlic cloves, crushed	**salt (to taste)**
1 large onion, roughly chopped	**2 tbsp fresh coriander, chopped**
2 tomatoes, roughly chopped	

Combine minced beef with fish sauce and black pepper, and let it stand for 10 minutes or more.

Heat oil in a pan over medium heat, and stir-fry garlic until lightly golden. Add onion and stir-fry for a couple of minutes. Add tomatoes and carrot, and cook for a few minutes until slightly softened.

Then add minced beef, and turn heat to high. Stir-fry until meat is browned, taking care to break up any lumps. Add potatoes and stock, and bring to a boil. Reduce heat, and simmer, *uncovered,* for about 30 minutes until the potatoes are cooked, stirring occasionally. Adjust seasoning to taste, if necessary.

Sprinkle with coriander, and serve immediately. ***Serves 3-4***

Handy tips

Meat: beef

How about .. serving it with loads of steamed rice. For variation, replace the onion with 6-8 spring onions, chopped

Larb

Here's a recipe for this popular Thai dish with ingredients that you can get from your local supermarket! And it comes with a seal of approval from my Thai friend. Feel free to replace the iceberg lettuce with another lettuce that takes your fancy (e.g. butter lettuce or red oak). And if you can get hold of roasted rice powder (khao koor), you won't have to make your own.

2 tbsp long grain white rice, uncooked	3-4 tbsp fresh mint leaves, chopped
	1-2 small red chillies, finely chopped
500g minced chicken, beef or pork	2-3 tbsp fish sauce
3 tbsp fresh lime juice	4 large iceberg lettuce leaves, washed and dried
2 tbsp spring onions, finely chopped	
2 tbsp Asian shallots (or eshallots), finely chopped	handful of fresh coriander (for garnish - optional)

Heat a pan over medium heat. (Do not use a non-stick pan for this.) Dry roast the rice for about 10-15 minutes or until it turns golden. Remove from pan, and crush into a coarse powder using a mortar and pestle or a spice/meat grinder.

In a separate pan over medium heat, cook minced meat with 2 tablespoons of lime juice until done, stirring frequently to break up any lumps. Remove from heat, and combine with ground rice, the remaining lime juice (1 tablespoon), spring onions, shallots, mint, chillies, and fish sauce. Mix thoroughly.

Place the lettuce leaves on serving plates. Spoon meat mixture onto the leaves, and garnish with coriander (if using). Serve immediately. ***Serves 4 as a starter***

Handy tips

Meat: chicken / beef / pork

How about .. serving it with white rice as a main meal for 2-3

Thai-style meatball salad

You're unlikely to find this fusion dish in Thailand but it came to me highly recommended by a friend. For the meatballs, I've added roasted coriander and cumin seeds ground up in a mortar and pestle. This gives them an exquisite aroma and makes them simply irresistible. If you don't have a mortar and pestle, use the packaged ground coriander and cumin from the supermarket instead. You'd lose out a little on the taste of the meatballs, but the overall dish will still be scrumptious!

150g mixed salad leaves

1 Lebanese cucumber, thinly sliced

125g cherry tomatoes, halved

½ small red onion, thinly sliced (optional)

For the meatballs:

1 tsp coriander seeds

1 tsp cumin seeds

600g lean minced beef or chicken

⅓ cup fresh coriander, chopped

1 egg, lightly beaten

¼ tsp salt (or to taste)

vegetable oil (for frying)

For the dressing:

80ml (⅓ cup) light olive oil

40ml (2 tbsp) fish sauce

2 tbsp fresh lime juice

1 tsp lime zest, grated

1 small red chilli (optional)

⅓ cup fresh coriander, finely chopped

⅓ cup fresh mint leaves, finely chopped

1 tbsp brown sugar

To make the meatballs, dry roast the coriander and cumin seeds in a small pan for several minutes. (Do not use a non-stick pan for this). They're ready when they give off a lovely aroma. Grind the roasted seeds in a mortar and pestle, and combine well with the rest of the ingredients (except oil) using your hands. (If you wish to check seasoning, fry a small lump of meat mixture – taste and adjust.) Shape level tablespoons of meat mixture into balls. Set aside and allow to stand for 15 minutes or more.

> **Handy tips**
> **Meat**: beef / chicken

In a frying-pan (preferably non-stick), heat oil and fry meatballs until browned all over and cooked through. Do not crowd the pan – fry in batches, if necessary. Drain on paper towels, and cool.

To make the dressing, put all ingredients in a jar with a lid, and shake well to combine.

In a large bowl, place salad leaves, cucumber, tomatoes and onion (if using), and toss them together with about half of the salad dressing. Divide into portions and place each on a serving plate.

In a separate bowl, place the cooked meatballs and add the remaining half of the salad dressing. Toss gently to coat the meatballs in dressing. Then arrange them on top of the salad, and serve immediately. ***Serves 4***

Smoky eggplant stir-fry

This Vietnamese dish has a kick from the chillies which marries beautifully with the distinctive, smoky flavour from eggplants charred over an open flame. Charring the eggplants is really the only complicated part – everything else is easy as pie!

2 large eggplants	**1-2 small red chillies, finely chopped**
2 tbsp vegetable oil	**500g minced beef or pork**
3-4 garlic cloves, crushed	**2 tbsp fish sauce**
3 Asian shallots (or eschalots), finely chopped	**salt and white pepper**

Hold the eggplants over an open flame on a gas stove or a barbecue with tongs, and turn them regularly to char their skins all over. Cool very briefly for 30 seconds, then put them in a plastic bag to sweat for 3-4 minutes.

Hold the eggplants by their stems under a running tap for a few minutes to cool even further. Peel off and discard their skins. Squeeze away excess water, and chop eggplants roughly.

In a wok or large frying-pan, heat oil over high heat until it is very hot or smoking. Add garlic, shallots and chillies. Fry very briefly for 30 seconds until they turn golden. Add minced meat, and stir-fry for another few minutes until browned, taking care to break up any lumps.

> **Handy tips**
>
> **Meat**: beef / pork
>
> **How about** .. serving it with baguette or crusty bread instead of steamed rice

Add fish sauce and the chopped eggplants, and stir to combine. Turn heat to low. Cover, and cook gently for 15-20 minutes or until eggplants soften. Season with salt and pepper, and serve with steamed rice. ***Serves 4***

Satays

In this Balinese recipe, deep-fried spring onions and coconut cream are mixed in with the meat, making it sweetly aromatic, and fabulous-tasting! If you don't like it spicy, feel free to leave out the red chillies altogether.

8-12 bamboo skewers, presoaked for 30 minutes or more before use

vegetable oil (for grilling)

For the satays:

3 large garlic cloves, roughly chopped

1-3 small red chillies, chopped

½ tsp salt (or to taste)

juice of a kaffir (or regular) lime

2 tsp ground turmeric

2 tbsp brown sugar

vegetable oil

5 spring onions, finely chopped

50ml coconut cream (or thick coconut milk)

500g minced beef or chicken

To make the satays, pound garlic, chillies and salt into a paste using a mortar and pestle. (If you don't have a mortar and pestle, put the garlic and chillies on a chopping board, sprinkle over with salt, and chop finely. Then mash into a coarse paste using the blade of the knife or the back of a spoon.) Add lime juice, turmeric and sugar. Mix well, and set aside.

Heat about 2cm of oil in a pan, and deep-fry spring onions until crisp and golden. Remove from pan, and drain on paper towels.

> **Handy tips**
>
> **Meat**: beef / chicken
>
> **How about** .. saving the oil that the spring onions have been fried in and use that for other stir-fries

Combine the garlic-turmeric paste, fried onions and coconut cream with the minced meat. Mix well using your hands. (If you wish to check seasoning, fry a small lump of meat mixture – taste and adjust.) Cover and refrigerate for 1 hour or more. Shape meat mixture into small sausages around one end of the bamboo skewers. (You may wish to moisten your hands with cold water for easier handling of meat mixture.)

Brush with oil, and grill/barbecue for 4-5 minutes each side or until cooked through. Turn only once, using tongs. *Serves 5-6 as a starter; Serves 3-4 as a main meal*

Kofta in coconut curry

These meatballs are lightly browned, and then cooked gently in a piquant, curry sauce flavoured with spices and coconut cream. You can adjust the spiciness of the dish to your liking by skipping or adding more chillies.

For the kofta:

500g minced lamb or beef

1 green chilli, seeded and finely chopped (optional)

2 garlic cloves, crushed

1 small onion, finely chopped

1 tsp fresh ginger, grated

1 egg

¼ tsp salt

vegetable oil (for frying)

For the curry sauce:

1 tbsp vegetable oil

1 onion, sliced

2 garlic cloves, crushed

2 tsp fresh ginger, grated

1-2 green chillies, finely chopped

1 tsp ground turmeric

1 tbsp ground coriander

3 tsp ground cumin

6 cardamom pods, lightly crushed (optional)

juice of ½ lemon

180ml (¾ cup) coconut milk

250ml (1 cup) lamb (or beef) stock

salt (to taste)

To make the kofta, combine all ingredients (except oil), and mix well using your hands. Shape tablespoons of meat mixture into balls.

Heat oil in a frying-pan (preferably non-stick) with a lid to fit, and quickly fry kofta until lightly browned all over. Do not crowd the pan – fry in batches, if necessary. Remove from pan, and drain on paper towels. Clean the pan.

> **Handy tips**
>
> **Meat**: lamb / beef

To make the curry sauce, heat oil over low heat. Add onion, garlic, ginger, chillies and turmeric, and stir-fry for about 5 minutes or until onion softens. Add coriander, cumin, cardamom (if using), lemon juice, coconut milk and stock. Stir to combine, and bring sauce to a simmering point. Drop kofta gently into the sauce. Cover and simmer for about 30 minutes, stirring occasionally to turn over kofta and coat evenly in sauce. Adjust seasoning to taste, if necessary, and serve with rice or Indian breads. ***Serves 3-4**

Indian kofta

There are many recipes for Indian kofta. They all have subtle differences in their spice-and-herb blend, and while some are dry, others are served with a sauce. The recipe I've chosen here is a relatively simple one. You can mould the meat mixture into the shape of little sausages around one end of the bamboo sticks so that they can be rotated individually and cooked to perfection. But if you're short of time, simply combine all ingredients and make them into flat meatballs or rissoles. They will still be beautiful!

8-12 bamboo skewers, presoaked in water for 30 minutes or more before use

vegetable oil (for grilling/ frying)

For the kofta:

500g minced chicken, lamb or beef

1 small onion, grated

1 small green (or red) chilli, finely chopped (optional)

2 tbsp fresh mint (or coriander) leaves, finely chopped

1 tsp fresh ginger, grated

1 tsp fresh garlic, crushed

2 tsp garam masala

½ tsp salt (or to taste)

To make the kofta, combine minced meat with all remaining ingredients. Using your hands, knead mixture for 3-4 minutes until stiff and smooth. (If you wish to check seasoning, fry a small lump of meat mixture – taste and adjust.) Cover and refrigerate for 1 hour or more.

Shape meat mixture into small sausages around one end of the bamboo skewers. (You may wish to moisten your hands with cold water for easier handling of meat mixture.)

Brush with oil, and grill/barbecue or pan-fry, turning only once. ***Serves 3-4***

> ### *Handy tips*
>
> **Meat**: chicken / lamb / beef
>
> **How about** .. serving them in naan bread or wraps and salad greens. They'll go well with raita, or even tzatziki (either homemade or straight off the supermarket shelf). They're a great starter if you're entertaining!

Indian Seekh kebabs

This is like an Indian version of sausages. The addition of dhal gives the kebab a distinctive flavour and texture. Using a high fat-content meat (20% or more) will keep the meat moist, particularly if you're putting it on the barbecue. However, if you're more health-conscious, use a leaner grade by all means – it'll still taste stunning! In India, the meat mixture is moulded onto flat, metal skewers but I've opted for bamboo skewers here because of their easy accessibility.

10-12 bamboo skewers, presoaked for 30 minutes or more before use

olive oil (for grilling)

lemon wedges (to serve)

1 small red onion, thinly sliced (to serve – optional)

For the dhal:

½ tsp ground turmeric

½ cup dried yellow split peas

For the kebabs:

1 tsp cumin seeds

600g minced lamb

2 garlic cloves, crushed

3 tbsp fresh coriander, chopped

2 tbsp spring onions, finely chopped

2 tsp fresh ginger, grated

¾ tsp freshly ground black pepper (or to taste)

¼ - ½ tsp cayenne pepper

1 tsp salt (or to taste)

To make the dhal, place turmeric and split peas in a pan. Add enough water to cover split peas by about 2cm, and bring to a boil. Reduce heat and simmer, *uncovered,* for 15-20 minutes or until the peas are tender but not mushy. (They're ready when you can crush one between your fingers.) Drain and set aside to cool. Then grind to a coarse meal in a food processor or spice/meat grinder.

> **Handy tips**
> **Meat**: lamb
> **How about** .. serving it with naan or other Indian breads and chutney

To make the kebabs, dry roast cumin seeds in a small pan over medium-low heat for 3-5 minutes. (Do not use a non-stick pan for this.) Shake the pan occasionally to prevent sticking. Combine roasted cumin seeds with the dhal, minced lamb, and all remaining ingredients. Using your hands, knead and squeeze the meat mixture for 3-4 minutes. (If you wish to check seasoning, fry a small lump of meat mixture – taste and adjust.) Cover and refrigerate for 1 hour or more.

Divide the meat mixture into 10-12 roughly equal portions. Shape each portion around one end of the skewers to form sausages about 12 cm long. (You may wish to moisten your hands with cold water for easier handling of meat mixture.)

Brush generously with oil, and grill/barbecue for 4-6 minutes each side or until cooked through. Turn only once, using tongs. Serve with lemon wedges, and red onion (if using). ***Serves 4***

Kofta curry

These succulent meatballs are flavoured with herbs and spices, and then cooked in an aromatic curry sauce. You could easily adjust the 'heat' by leaving out the chilli altogether or by adding 1-2 more (with seeds left in).

For the kofta:	For the curry sauce:
500g minced beef or lamb	**2 tbsp vegetable oil**
2 garlic cloves, crushed	**2 garlic cloves, crushed**
1 small onion, finely chopped	**1 onion, finely chopped**
1 tbsp fresh coriander, finely chopped	**1-2 green or red chillies, finely chopped**
2 tsp ground cumin	**3 tbsp curry powder**
1 tsp garam masala	**4 cardamom pods, lightly crushed**
1 tsp ground coriander	**500ml (2 cups) beef stock**
1 tsp ground turmeric	**1 tbsp fresh coriander, finely chopped**
1 tbsp plain yoghurt	**1 tbsp tomato paste**
3 tbsp plain flour	**2 tbsp plain yoghurt**
1 egg	
½ tsp salt (or to taste)	
black pepper	

To make the kofta, combine all ingredients and mix well using your hands. Shape tablespoons of meat mixture into balls, and set aside. (You may wish to moisten your hands with cold water for easier handling of meat mixture.)

> **Handy tips**
>
> **Meat**: beef / lamb
>
> **How about** .. serving it on a bed of fluffy white rice or with some warm naan bread

To make the curry sauce, heat oil over medium-low heat. Add garlic, onion and chillies, and fry for about 5 minutes or until onion is soft but not browned. Reduce heat, and add curry powder and cardamom pods. Stir-fry for 2-3 minutes. Gradually stir in stock, and add coriander, tomato paste and yoghurt. Stir to mix well, and bring to a simmering point. Cover and simmer for 10 minutes.

Drop meatballs gently into the sauce – a few at a time, allowing them to harden a little before adding more. Simmer, *uncovered*, for another 20 minutes or until meatballs are cooked through. If possible, avoid stirring (you could shake the pan from time to time to prevent sticking). Simmer a little longer if the curry is too thin or add a little more stock if it is too dry. ***Serves 3-4***

Easy pilaf

A tasty meal for you to whip up in less than an hour! If you don't have all the spices in stock, use two tablespoons of good-quality curry powder instead.

1-2 tbsp vegetable oil	**300g (1½ cups) long grain rice**
1 onion, finely chopped	**750ml (3 cups) beef or chicken stock (or ½ stock, ½ water)**
2 garlic cloves, crushed	
2 tsp ground turmeric	**salt (to taste)**
3 tsp ground coriander	**100g (²⁄₃ cup) frozen green peas**
3 tsp ground cumin	**2 tbsp fresh mint or coriander, chopped**
500g minced beef, chicken or lamb	

In a large pan with a lid to fit, heat oil over medium heat. Add onion and garlic, and fry until onion softens. Add turmeric, coriander and cumin and fry for about a minute. Add minced meat, and fry until browned, taking care to break up any lumps.

Stir in rice and stock, and season with salt (if necessary). Bring to a simmering point. Then cover and simmer for about 25 minutes, or until rice is just cooked, stirring occasionally to prevent sticking.

Add peas, and stir to mix well. Simmer for another 5 minutes. Stir in chopped mint, and serve. ***Serves 4***

Handy tips

Meat: beef / chicken / lamb

How about .. adding a chopped tomato with the peas

Other Starters and Main Meals

Middle East and Africa

Middle Eastern kofta

Kofta, in one form or another, is ubiquitous in the Middle East, and recipes abound for this dish. Before the onset of technology, people used to pound the meat with herbs and spices in a mortar and pestle. Now it's much easier in a food processor. But if you don't want to do any of these, simply grate the onion, chop the coriander finely, and combine thoroughly with the meat and spices using your hands. If you're putting the kofta on a BBQ, consider using a fattier meat (with 15-20% fat) to keep it moist.

500g minced lamb or beef (or ½ lamb, ½ beef)

1 medium onion, roughly chopped

1 cup fresh coriander leaves, roughly chopped

1 tsp ground cumin

1 tsp paprika

½ tsp freshly ground black pepper

½ tsp salt (or to taste)

olive oil (for grilling/frying)

Place all ingredients (except oil) in a food processor or meat/spice grinder, and blend until smooth. (If you wish to check seasoning, fry a small lump of meat mixture – taste and adjust.) Cover and refrigerate for 1 hour or more. Shape meat mixture into meatballs or small, flat sausages. (You may wish to moisten your hands with cold water for easier handling of meat mixture.)

Brush with oil, and grill/barbecue or pan-fry, turning only once. ***Serves 5-6 as a starter; Serves 3-4 as a main meal***

Handy tips

Meat: lamb / beef

How about .. serving them with pita bread, tabouli salad and dollops of hommus or baba ghanoush

Turkish kofta

These sensational meatballs are soft and luscious! The currants, pine nuts, herbs and spices all combine to give them a depth of flavours and a richness of textures. Serve them on a special occasion and watch them go down like a treat! If you don't have the means to crumb bread, simple use $1/3$ cup of dry breadcrumbs instead.

sprigs of parsley (for garnish)	**2 tbsp pine nuts**
lemon wedges (to serve)	**2 tbsp flat-leaf parsley, finely chopped**
For the kofta:	**2 tbsp fresh dill, finely chopped**
2-3 tbsp currants	**1 tsp paprika**
400g lean minced lamb	**1 egg, lightly beaten**
1 small red onion, finely chopped	**¾ tsp salt (or to taste)**
2 garlic cloves, crushed	**freshly ground black pepper**
2 tsp ground cinnamon	**vegetable oil (for grilling/frying)**
2 slices sandwich bread (white or wholemeal), crumbed	

To make the kofta, soak currants in warm water for 5-10 minutes. Drain and set aside. Put minced lamb, onion, garlic and cinnamon in a large bowl. Knead and squeeze the mixture with your hands for 3-4 minutes. Add all remaining ingredients (except oil), and mix thoroughly. (If you wish to check seasoning, fry a small lump of meat mixture – taste and adjust.) Cover and refrigerate for 1 hour or more.

Shape tablespoons of meat mixture into oval-shaped meatballs or small, flat sausages. (You may wish to moisten your hands with cold water for easier handling of meat mixture.)

> *Handy tips*
>
> **Meat**: lamb
>
> **How about** .. serving it with pita bread, sliced red onion, salad leaves and thick yoghurt mixed with aioli/garlic sauce

Brush with oil and grill/barbecue or pan-fry, turning only once. Garnish with parsley, and serve with lemon wedges. ***Serves 5-7 as a starter; Serves 3-4 as a main meal***

Iraqi chicken kofta

With the addition of spices and two different capsicums (red and green), these minced chicken kebabs not only look great but taste fabulous! In the Middle East, kebabs are cooked on flat and long metal skewers. If you're planning to grill the meat, you could shape the meat mixture into a sausage around the blade of a (blunt) knife from your cutlery set, then pull the knife out from the middle, and place the kofta directly on the wire rack of your grill.

500g minced chicken	**½ tsp white pepper**
1 garlic clove, crushed	**3 tbsp green capsicum, chopped**
1 tsp ground cumin	**3 tbsp red capsicum, chopped**
½ to 1 tsp paprika	**3 tbsp flat-leaf parsley, chopped**
½ tsp salt (or to taste)	**olive oil (for grilling/frying)**

To make the kofta, place minced chicken, garlic, cumin, paprika, salt and pepper in a food processor, and process into a coarse paste. Add green capsicum, red capsicum and parsley, and pulse until just combined. (If you wish to check seasoning, fry a small lump of meat mixture – taste and adjust.)

Shape meat mixture into meatballs or small, flat sausages. (You may wish to moisten your hands with cold water for easier handling of meat mixture.)

Brush with oil, and grill/barbecue or pan-fry, turning only once. ***Serves 3-4***

> *Handy tips*
>
> **Meat**: chicken
>
> **How about** .. serving it with fluffy white rice mixed with 1-2 tbsp butter

Kofta in tomato sauce

There are numerous versions of this popular Middle Eastern dish. The addition of breadcrumbs in this recipe makes the koftas lovely and tender. But if you don't mind putting in extra time and effort, you could replace the breadcrumbs with cooked eggplant or zucchini – a practice which is common in the Middle East.

For the kofta:

500g minced lamb or beef (or ½ lamb, ½ beef)

2 tbsp dry breadcrumbs

1-2 tbsp onion, grated

2 tbsp flat-leaf parsley, finely chopped

1 tbsp fresh mint, finely chopped

1 tsp ground cumin

½ tsp salt (or to taste)

black pepper

vegetable oil (for frying)

For the tomato sauce:

2 tbsp vegetable oil

1 onion, grated

½ to 1 tsp ground turmeric

½ tsp ground ginger (optional)

juice of ½ lemon

2 tbsp flat-leaf parsley, finely chopped

2 x 400g tins whole tomatoes

1 tbsp tomato paste

salt and black pepper

To make the kofta, combine all ingredients (except oil). Mix well and knead, using your hands. Shape heaped tablespoons of mixture into meatballs or finger-shaped rissoles.

In a frying-pan (preferably non-stick), heat oil and quickly fry kofta until lightly browned all over. Do not crowd the pan – fry in batches, if necessary. Drain kofta on paper towels, and set aside.

> *Handy tips*
>
> **Meat**: lamb / beef
>
> **How about** .. serving it with rice and green beans (steamed or lightly boiled)

To make the tomato sauce, heat oil in a large pan over medium heat. Fry onion for a few minutes until it begins to brown. Stir in turmeric and ginger (if using), and fry very briefly for 30 seconds. Add lemon juice, parsley, tomatoes and tomato paste, and season with salt and pepper. Stir to mix, and break up the tomatoes. Then drop kofta gently into the tomato sauce. Cover, and simmer over low heat for 30 minutes, stirring occasionally to turn the kofta over and coat them evenly with sauce. ***Serves 3-4***

Stuffed capsicums with tomato sauce

This is a gorgeous Middle Eastern dish of capsicums stuffed with meat and rice, flavoured with herb and spices, and then baked in a tomato sauce! The contrast in colours between the green (of the capsicums) and the reds (of the tomato sauce and capsicums) is lovely, and gives this dish a striking presentation!

½ cup short (or medium) grain rice, washed

1 tbsp olive oil

1 small onion, finely chopped

250g lean minced lamb or beef

2 tbsp pine nuts

1 tomato, peeled and chopped (optional)

2 tbsp flat-leaf parsley, finely chopped

¼ tsp ground cinnamon (or ¼ tsp ground allspice)

salt and black pepper

6 medium capsicums (any mix of red and green)

For the tomato sauce:

1 x 400g tin chopped tomatoes

125ml (½ cup) water

1 tbsp olive oil

salt and pepper

Cover rice in plenty of cold water, and cook for about 10 minutes or until almost done. Drain well, and set aside.

Preheat oven to 180C (conventional). Over medium heat, heat oil in a pan with a lid to fit. Add onion, and fry for a few minutes until softened. Add minced meat, and fry until browned, taking care to break up any lumps. Then add the cooked rice, ½ a cup of water, pine nuts, tomato (if using), parsley and cinnamon. Season with salt and pepper, and bring to a boil before reducing heat. Cover and simmer stuffing mixture gently for 10 minutes.

> ### Handy tips
>
> **Meat**: lamb / beef
>
> **How about** .. adding 1-2 tbsp sultanas or currants to the stuffing for variation

Slice the tops off capsicums, and reserve for use. Discard seeds and membranes. (If a capsicum is not standing upright, cut a thin slice off its base.) Fill capsicums with the stuffing mixture, and place tops back on capsicums. (Do not fill the vegetables to the brim as the rice expands during cooking.) Place capsicums in a baking dish wide enough to hold the capsicums in a single layer.

Make the tomato sauce by combining all ingredients, and pour it all over the capsicums. Cover with foil (or lid), and bake in pre-heated oven for 25-30 minutes. Then bake, *uncovered,* for another 15 minutes, and serve with rice or Lebanese bread. **Serves 3-4**

Lebanese kibbeh

This is a tried-and-true family recipe from my friend of Lebanese descent. Kibbeh is like a Lebanese version of meatloaf, and is great eaten hot or cold. With an exquisite mix of herbs and spices, it's really home-cooking at its best – delicious, nutritious and easy to prepare!

½ cup fine-grade crushed/cracked wheat	**2 tsp fresh mint leaves, finely chopped**
2 tbsp pine nuts	**2 tbsp water**
olive oil	**¾ tsp salt (or to taste)**
500g lean minced beef or lamb	**¼ tsp ground cinnamon**
1 medium onion, finely chopped	**¼ tsp ground nutmeg (or allspice)**
2 tbsp flat-leaf parsley, finely chopped	**¼ tsp ground black pepper**

Soak crushed wheat in cold water for about 1 hour. Drain well, and squeeze away excess liquid until as dry as possible.

Preheat oven to 180C (conventional), and grease a square baking dish (about 21cm) or round baking dish (about 23cm). In a frying-pan, lightly brown the pine nuts in a little oil, and set aside. Using your hands, combine crushed wheat with minced meat, onion, parsley, mint, water, salt and all the spices. Spread roughly half of the meat mixture across the base of the baking dish. Sprinkle pine nuts evenly all over, and cover with the remaining half of the meat mixture.

> ### Handy tips
>
> **Meat**: beef / lamb
>
> **How about** .. serving it with pita bread (or lavash), yoghurt and tabouli (or a hot veggie dish)

Brush the top of the kibbeh with oil. With a knife, make cuts of 4 cm squares or diamond shapes into the *kibbeh*. Bake in pre-heated oven for 30-35 minutes, or until browned and cooked through. Serve from the dish, or invert onto a serving platter. ***Serves 3-4***

Persian chicken pilaf

This dish is a real winner with a distinctive orange fragrance, and morsels of meat flavoured with the natural sweetness of dried apricots!

300g (1½ cups) long grain rice, washed

35g (⅓ cup) blanched almonds, halved lengthwise

2 tbsp extra virgin olive oil

500g minced chicken

salt and freshly ground black pepper

40g (2 tbsp) butter

1 large onion, finely chopped

750mls (3 cups) chicken stock (or ½ stock, ½ water)

⅔ cup (100g) dried apricots, chopped

1 tbsp orange zest, grated

1-2 tbsp flat leaf parsley, chopped (optional)

In a large bowl, put rice and enough water to cover it by 2cm or so. Soak for about 30 minutes. Drain well and set aside.

Dry roast almonds in a pan until lightly golden. (Do not use a non-stick pan for this.) Set aside for later use.

In a large pan, heat oil over medium heat. Add minced chicken and fry until cooked and *dry*, taking care to break up any lumps. Season with salt and black pepper. Remove from pan and set aside. Heat butter in the pan, and fry onion until lightly browned. Add the rice, and cook for 5 minutes until it turns almost chalky white, stirring frequently.

> **Handy tips**
> **Meat**: chicken

Add stock, apricots, orange zest, and return minced chicken to the pan. Bring to a boil, and adjust seasoning to taste, if necessary. Reduce heat, and allow to bubble gently, *uncovered,* for about 10 minutes, or until the surface liquid has evaporated. Cover the pan, and cook over very low heat for another 10 minutes. (If you wish to observe the traditional method, wrap the lid of the pan with a dish towel, and fold the edges up over the top of the lid. The cloth absorbs steam from the rice during cooking, and stops moisture from dripping back down onto the rice.) Remove from heat, and rest, *covered*, for another 5-10 minutes.

Sprinkle with parsley (if using) and the roasted almonds. Serve immediately.
Serves 4-5

Moroccan kofta with tomatoes and eggs

Slightly different variations of this Moroccan dish can be found in many cookbooks on North African cuisines. The version I've chosen is simple and easy. Meatballs and eggs make perfect partners – together, they turn this dish into a hearty meal enjoyed by one and all. I haven't used breadcrumbs in this recipe as they already feature in many other recipes in this book. But if you prefer your meatballs to be soft and moist, then feel free to add 2-3 tablespoons of dry breadcrumbs to the meat mixture.

600g minced lamb or beef	For the tomato sauce:
2 garlic cloves, crushed	**1 x 400g tin chopped tomatoes**
¼ cup fresh coriander, chopped	**1 tbsp tomato paste**
1 tsp ground cumin	**1 tbsp liquid honey**
½ to 1 tsp paprika	**1 tsp ground cumin**
¼ tsp cayenne pepper (optional)	**80ml (⅓ cup) hot water**
½ tsp salt (or to taste)	**salt and black pepper**
black pepper	
olive oil (for frying)	
4 eggs	

To make the tomato sauce, combine all ingredients in a bowl, and set aside.

To make the meatballs, combine minced meat with garlic, coriander, cumin, paprika, cayenne pepper (if using), salt and pepper. Mix well using your hands, and shape heaped tablespoons of meat mixture into balls.

In a large frying-pan (preferably non-stick) with a lid to fit, heat a little oil, and quickly fry meatballs until lightly browned all over. Do not crowd the pan – fry in batches, if necessary. When all the meatballs are lightly browned, return them to the pan, and pour tomato sauce on top. Cover and simmer over low heat for 20-30 minutes, stirring occasionally to turn the meatballs over and coat them evenly with sauce.

Handy tips

Meat: lamb / beef

How about .. serving it with couscous and a tomato salad or cooked carrots tossed in a honey and olive oil dressing with a pinch of ground cumin

Break the eggs individually into the sauce, making sure they are separate and apart from each other. Cook for another 5 minutes or until the egg whites are just set and the yolks are still soft. Serve directly from the pan at the table.
Serves 4

Bobotie

This is a popular dish in South Africa where most home cooks would have his/her own favourite recipe. It's reminiscent of another baked mince dish from Russia (see page 49) which makes one marvel at the paths culinary influences take across geographies and cultural boundaries.

1 tbsp vegetable oil	1 tbsp lemon juice
1 onion, sliced	2 tsp curry powder
1 slice sandwich bread (white or wholemeal)	1-2 tsp sugar
	½ tsp ground turmeric
125ml (½ cup) milk	½ tsp salt (or to taste)
500g lean minced beef	¼ tsp ground black pepper
¼ cup sultanas (or 6-8 blanched almonds, chopped)	1 egg
1 tbsp fruit chutney (optional)	2-3 bay leaves (for garnish)

Preheat oven to 180C (conventional), and grease a baking dish. Heat oil in a pan over medium heat, and fry onion for several minutes until softened. Remove from heat and set aside. Soak bread in half the milk (¼ cup) for about 10 minutes. Squeeze dry over a bowl, and reserve the milk for later use.

Combine the cooked onion with the bread mixture, minced beef, sultanas, chutney (if using), lemon juice, curry powder, sugar, turmeric, salt and pepper. Mix well, and spread the meat mixture out in the baking dish.

Beat egg with the remaining milk (¼ cup), and the milk reserved from the bread. Pour over the top of the meat mixture, and garnish with bay leaves. Bake in pre-heated oven for 30-35 minutes.
Serves 3-4

> **Handy tips**
>
> **Meat**: beef
>
> **How about** .. serving it with 'yellow' steamed rice cooked with a little added turmeric

Other Starters and Main Meals

Europe and The Americas

Greek meatballs in tomato sauce

These succulent meatballs with green olives are browned, and then cooked in a gorgeous tomato sauce. If you think tomato sauce is just tomato sauce, then think again! The one in this recipe simply bursts with flavours from the different spices, and has all my dinner guests bedazzled! If, unlike me, you'd like a more subtle flavouring from the spices, try wrapping them in muslin instead.

For the meatballs:

2 slices sandwich bread (white or wholemeal), crusts removed

180ml (¾ cup) dry white wine

500g lean minced lamb (preferably twice minced)

50g green olives, pitted and chopped

1 small onion, finely chopped

3-4 garlic cloves, crushed

1 tbsp ground cumin

1 egg, lightly beaten

½ tsp salt (or to taste)

freshly ground black pepper

plain flour (for coating)

olive oil (for frying)

For the tomato sauce:

1 x 700g jar tomato passata

1 x 400g tin whole tomatoes

2-3 cloves (optional)

2 bay leaves

2 cinnamon sticks

2 tsp cumin seeds

1 tsp sugar

3 tbsp olive oil

50g green olives, pitted and sliced

To make the meatballs, soak bread in wine for about 15 minutes. Then squeeze until almost dry over a bowl, and reserve wine for later use. Combine bread mixture with minced lamb, olives, onion, garlic, cumin and egg. Season with salt and pepper. (If you wish to check seasoning, fry a small lump of meat mixture – taste and adjust.) Shape tablespoons of meat mixture into balls, and coat lightly in flour. Cover and set aside or refrigerate while you prepare the sauce.

> **Handy tips**
>
> **Meat**: lamb
>
> **How about** .. serving it with plenty of white rice, and a Greek salad

To make the tomato sauce, combine all ingredients (except olives) in a pan large enough for the sauce and meatballs. Stir in reserved wine and break up the tomatoes. Bring sauce to a simmering point. Cover and simmer over low heat for about 45 minutes.

In a frying-pan (preferably non-stick), heat oil over medium heat, and quickly fry meatballs until lightly browned all over. Do not crowd the pan – fry in batches, if necessary.

When the tomato sauce is ready, drop meatballs gently into the sauce, and add sliced olives. Simmer over low heat for another 15 minutes, stirring once or twice to turn meatballs over to coat them evenly in sauce. Remove cinnamon sticks and bay leaves from the sauce before serving. ***Serves 4***

Moussaka

There are countless recipes for this wonderful, traditional Greek dish. The one I've chosen here uses a ratio of 1:1 for the quantities of meat versus eggplant. But there are other recipes advocating a ratio of 1:2 so feel free to make your own adaptation. If your kids don't like eggplants, you can replace them with zucchinis – either way, they'll find these veggies hard to resist as they are mixed in with a creamy, cheese sauce.

olive oil

2 onions, finely chopped

3-4 garlic cloves, crushed

1 kg lean minced lamb or beef

60ml (¼ cup) white wine

1 x 400g tin chopped tomatoes

1 tbsp fresh oregano, chopped

1 cinnamon stick (optional)

salt and black pepper

1 kg eggplant (2-3 large eggplants)

For the cheese sauce:

80g (4 tbsp) butter

75g (½ cup) plain flour

625ml (2½ cups) hot milk

50g Parmesan cheese, grated

¼ tsp grated nutmeg (optional)

2 eggs, lightly beaten

Heat 2 tablespoons of oil over medium-high heat, and fry onions and garlic for a few minutes until lightly golden. Add minced meat, and fry until browned, taking care to break up any lumps. Add wine, tomatoes, oregano and cinnamon (if using). Season with salt and pepper. Turn heat to low, and simmer for 30-40 minutes. (Remove cinnamon stick from meat sauce, if necessary.)

Preheat oven to 200C (conventional). Cut eggplants lengthways into slices of about 4-5mm thick. Heat plenty of oil in a pan over high heat, and add a layer of eggplant slices. (The more oil there is in the pan, and the hotter the oil, the less oil the eggplant will absorb.) Do not crowd the pan – do this in batches, if necessary. Fry all eggplant slices until they are slightly golden on both sides. Drain on paper towels.

Handy tips
Meat: lamb / beef

To make the cheese sauce, melt butter in a pan over medium heat. Add flour and stir for 1-2 minutes or until a smooth paste is formed. Remove from heat, and add hot milk gradually, stirring all the time to work the paste into the milk. Return to heat, and continue to stir until sauce boils and thickens. Stir in Parmesan and nutmeg (if using), and set aside to cool for about 5 minutes. Add eggs and mix well.

Spoon alternate layers of meat sauce and eggplant into a shallow ovenproof dish, and finish off with a layer of eggplant on top. Pour cheese sauce all over the top, and bake in pre-heated oven for 25-30 minutes or until golden. ***Serves 6***

Beef and mushroom risotto

Mushroom-lovers will find this recipe irresistible – it's richly aromatic, silky smooth and deeply satisfying!

1.25 litres (5 cups) chicken stock	250ml (1 cup) white wine
1 tbsp olive oil	200g button mushrooms, sliced
40g (2 tbsp) butter	75g (¾ cup) Parmesan cheese, grated
1 medium onion, finely chopped	
2 garlic cloves, crushed	⅓ cup flat-leaf parsley, finely chopped
350g minced beef	
2 cups Arborio rice, unwashed	

In a pan, bring stock to a boil. Reduce heat to low, and keep stock simmering very gently.

In a separate pan deep enough to hold the risotto, heat oil and half the butter (1 tablespoon) over medium heat. Fry onion and garlic for a few minutes until onion is lightly browned. Turn heat to high. Add minced beef, and fry until *dry* and browned, taking care to break up any lumps.

> **Handy tips**
>
> **Meat**: beef
>
> **How about** .. serving it with a salad of greens

Add rice and fry for a minute, stirring constantly. Pour in wine and bring to a boil. Reduce heat and simmer, stirring constantly, until the wine has been absorbed into the rice.

Add one-quarter of the hot stock, and stir until the stock is cooked into the rice before adding more stock. Repeat this process, adding remaining stock a-quarter at a time, and stirring until the liquid has been absorbed between additions.

Stir in mushrooms after half of the stock has been added. Continue until all stock has been added, and the rice is *al dente* (i.e. tender but firm). Remove from heat. Stir in Parmesan, parsley and the remaining butter (1 tablespoon). Cover with lid and allow it to sit for a couple of minutes. Serve immediately. **Serves 4**

Country-style risotto

This risotto is creamy, gorgeous and easy to make! It doesn't take as long as some of the other risotto recipes as the amount of stock and wine added are a bit less. So why pay $18 or more for a plate of risotto at a restaurant when you can make it at home for your family (3-4 people) for just $12?

1 litre (4 cups) chicken stock *($3.50)*

1 tbsp olive oil

1 small onion, finely chopped *(0.30)*

150g good quality Italian pork sausages, skinned and crumbled *($1.50)*

2 ¹/₃ cups Arborio rice, unwashed *($2.50)*

¹/₃ cup white wine *($1.50)*

1 tomato, peeled, seeded and diced *($0.30)*

handful of flat-leaf parsley, roughly chopped *($0.50)*

¹/₃ cup Parmesan cheese, grated *($2.00)*

20g (1 tbsp) butter

In a pan, bring stock to a boil. Reduce heat to low, and keep stock simmering very gently.

In a separate pan deep enough to hold the risotto, heat oil over medium heat. Fry onion for a couple of minutes until softened. Add sausage meat and rice. Fry for another 2-3 minutes, stirring constantly to prevent from sticking, and taking care to break up any lumps. Add wine and reduce heat to low. Stir constantly until the wine has been absorbed into the rice.

Add hot chicken stock a ladle at a time. Each time you add stock, give it a quick stir to mix it in with the rice, and allow the rice to absorb most of the stock before adding more.

After about 10 minutes, add tomato. Continue adding the remaining stock a ladle at a time, adding more only when most of the liquid has been absorbed.

> **Handy tips**
>
> **Meat**: pork
>
> **How about** .. replacing the tomato with a stalk of celery (finely chopped), for variation

When the rice is *al dente* (i.e. tender but firm), remove from heat. Add parsley, Parmesan and butter. Stir vigorously to whip and fluff up the risotto. Serve immediately. ***Serves 3-4***

Note: All prices shown were as at May 2009 in Sydney.

Chipolatas and lentils

Lentils are used in many Italian dishes, and are often coupled with sausages. In this recipe, minced pork flavoured with herbs is shaped into small sausages, then lightly browned and baked on a bed of lentils. It's a recipe from a friend who's an awesome cook, and it makes a fabulous meal that is great to share with friends.

1½ cups green lentils, washed	2 garlic cloves, crushed
2 onions (1 quartered and 1 finely chopped)	2 tsp fresh rosemary (or sage), finely chopped
1 garlic clove	1-2 tsp fresh thyme
sprig of thyme	1 egg
salt (to taste)	1 tsp salt (or to taste)
2 rashers bacon, finely chopped	freshly ground black pepper
For the chipolatas:	2 tbsp extra virgin olive oil (for frying)
800g minced pork	

Cover lentils in plenty of cold water, and allow to soak for 2 hours. Drain well, and set aside.

Preheat oven to 180C (conventional). To make the chipolatas, combine all ingredients (except oil), and mix well using your hands. (If you wish to check seasoning, fry a small lump of meat mixture – taste and adjust.) Shape meat mixture into chipolatas (6-7cm length).

> ### Handy tips
> **Meat**: pork
>
> **How about** .. serving them with mashed potatoes or crusty bread, and a leafy salad

Place lentils in a pan. Add quartered onion, garlic, thyme, salt, and enough water to cover generously. Bring to a boil before reducing heat. Cover and simmer for 15-20 minutes or until lentils are tender but not mushy. Drain well and remove onion, garlic and thyme.

In a frying-pan, (preferably non-stick), heat oil and lightly brown *chipolatas* on 2 sides. Do not crowd the pan – fry in batches, if necessary. Remove from pan, and set aside.

In the pan you've used to fry the chipolatas, add bacon and chopped onion, and fry for several minutes until bacon begins to crisp. Remove from pan, and combine with the cooked lentils. Spread lentil/bacon mixture over the base of a baking dish, and arrange chipolatas on top. Bake in pre-heated oven for 25-30 minutes or until chipolatas are cooked through. ***Serves 5-6***

Apple meatballs with wine

The unusual but fantastic meatballs in this Italian recipe have a hint of natural sweetness from the apples, and are incredibly moist and juicy! They're a real treat so make sure you have enough because they'll come back for more.

800g lean minced beef	**¾ tsp salt (or to taste)**
2 red apples (e.g. Pink Lady, Red Delicious), peeled and grated	**freshly ground black pepper**
	20g (1 tbsp) butter
2 tbsp flat-leaf parsley, finely chopped	**2 tbsp extra virgin olive oil**
2 large eggs	**125ml (½ cup) dry white wine**

Combine minced beef with grated apples, parsley, eggs, salt and black pepper. Mix well using your hands. (If you wish to check seasoning, fry a small lump of meat mixture – taste and adjust.) Shape heaped tablespoons of meat mixture into flat meatballs.

In a large frying-pan (preferably non-stick), heat butter and oil, and fry meatballs for 4-5 minutes each side or until cooked through. Do not crowd the pan – fry in batches, if necessary.

Tip away excess oil (if necessary), and return all meatballs to the pan. Add wine, and allow to bubble for a few minutes to reduce. Transfer meatballs to a serving platter, and pour wine juice on top. Serve immediately. ***Serves 5-6***

> *Handy tips*
>
> **Meat**: beef
>
> **How about** .. serving them with a green salad and white rice mixed with 1-2 tbsp tomato passata. Mashed potatoes will also go well with these meatballs

Lemon meatballs

Don't be deceived by the simplicity of this recipe. These Italian meatballs have a beautiful, lemony tang, and are lovely as starters if you're entertaining.

500g lean minced beef	**¼ tsp salt (or to taste)**
zest of ½ lemon, grated	**freshly ground black pepper**
65g (²/₃ cup) Parmesan cheese, grated	**butter (for frying)**
125ml (½ cup) thick (or double) cream	**juice of ½ lemon**

Combine minced beef with lemon zest, Parmesan and half the cream (¼ cup). Season with salt and pepper. Mix well using your hands. Shape level tablespoons of meat mixture into flat meatballs.

Heat butter in a frying-pan (preferably non-stick). Fry meatballs for 4-5 minutes each side or until cooked through. Do not crowd the pan - fry in batches, if necessary. Remove from pan and drain on paper towels, keeping warm, if possible.

> ### *Handy tips*
> **Meat**: beef
>
> **How about** .. serving them as a main meal with bread or mashed potatoes and a salad

Pour the remaining cream (¼ cup) into the pan you've used to fry the meatballs. Add lemon juice, and cook very briefly for about 30 seconds or until slightly thickened, stirring constantly. Pour cream sauce over meatballs, and serve immediately. ***Serves 4-5 as a starter***

Italian country meatballs with garden vegetables

Don't be put off by the long list of ingredients because this Italian dish is a truly sublime, one-dish meal to share with friends! It has a richness that is derived from a unique combination of a myriad of flavours and textures. You'll need good quality, dry breadcrumbs which are available from bakeries and specialty grocers.

250g green beans, trimmed and chopped (4cm lengths)

2 potatoes, cut into large chunks

3 slices pancetta (or bacon), finely chopped

1 onion, finely chopped

1 large garlic clove, finely chopped

125ml (½ cup) dry white wine

4 large ripe tomatoes, peeled and chopped

125ml (½ cup) chicken stock

1 bay leaf (preferably fresh)

pinch of ground cinnamon

salt and freshly ground black pepper

2 tbsp flat-leaf parsley, finely chopped

Parmesan cheese, grated (to serve)

For the meatballs:

350g minced beef

350g Italian pork sausages, skinned

120g (½ cup) ricotta cheese

50g (½ cup) Parmesan cheese, grated

¼ cup good quality dry breadcrumbs

⅓ cup dried currants

handful of pine nuts

pinch of ground cinnamon (optional)

1 large egg

2 tbsp dry white wine

1 large garlic clove, crushed

2 tbsp flat-leaf parsley, finely chopped

¼ tsp salt (or to taste)

freshly ground black pepper

extra virgin olive oil (for frying)

Blanch beans in salted, boiling water for about a minute. Remove and set aside. Add potatoes to the water, and cook until just tender. Remove and set aside.

To make the meatballs, combine all ingredients (except oil), and mix with your hands until ingredients are *just* combined. Do not overwork the mixture if you want your

> **Handy tips**
>
> **Meat**: beef & pork
>
> **How about** .. serving it with hot, crusty Italian rolls

meatballs to be light in texture. (If you wish to check seasoning, fry a small lump of meat mixture – taste and adjust.) Shape level tablespoons of meat mixture into balls.

In a frying-pan (preferably non-stick), heat oil over medium heat, and fry meatballs until well browned all over. Do not crowd the pan – fry in batches, if necessary. Remove from pan and drain on paper towels. Tip away all but 2 tablespoons of oil from the pan.

Add pancetta to the pan, and fry for several minutes until crisp. Add onion, and fry for another 3-4 minutes until softened. Add garlic, and fry for a couple of minutes or until slightly golden. Pour in wine and cook, *uncovered,* until reduced by half. Add tomatoes, stock, bay leaf, and cinnamon. Season with salt and pepper, and bring to a simmering point. Simmer*, uncovered,* over low heat for about 10 minutes to reduce. Add the cooked beans and potatoes, and stir gently to combine. Then add meatballs, and simmer for a further 5 minutes or until cooked through. Sprinkle with parsley, and serve with grated Parmesan.
Serves 4

Meatballs with sage and Marsala

These Italian meatballs are terrific! The Marsala wine gives them a light touch of sweet nuttiness that is reminiscent of chocolate, and makes them truly tempting. However, if you're not a fan of sweetness (in any guise), use dry Marsala or medium dry sherry instead.

750g lean minced beef	**½ tsp salt (or to taste)**
50g (½ cup) Parmesan cheese, grated	**freshly ground black pepper**
	extra butter (for frying)
12 large sage leaves, finely chopped	**125ml (½ cup) Marsala wine**
40g (2 tbsp) butter, melted	

Combine minced beef with Parmesan, sage, and melted butter. Season with salt and pepper. Mix well with your hands, and refrigerate for 30 minutes. (If you wish to check seasoning, fry a small lump of meat mixture – taste and adjust.) Shape heaped tablespoons of meat mixture into flat meatballs.

In a large frying-pan (preferably non-stick), heat a little butter over medium heat, and fry meatballs for 4-5 minutes each side or until cooked through. Do not crowd the pan – fry in batches, if necessary.

> ### *Handy tips*
> **Meat**: beef
>
> **How about** .. serving them with mashed potatoes and a green salad

Tip away excess oil (if necessary), and return all meatballs to the pan. Add wine, and allow it to bubble for a few minutes to reduce. Transfer meatballs to a serving platter, and pour wine juice on top. Serve immediately. ***Serves 4-5***

Italian potato croquettes

The potatoes in these yummy croquettes are mashed, and then mixed with minced meat, mortadella (or ham) and Parmesan. They are easy to make, and go nicely in picnic hampers, or served as lunch with a green salad.

2 large potatoes

350g lean minced beef, veal or chicken

3 slices mortadella (or ham), finely chopped

1 large egg, lightly beaten

2 tbsp Parmesan cheese, grated

2 tbsp flat-leaf parsley, finely chopped

¼ tsp salt (or to taste)

black pepper

dry breadcrumbs (for coating)

olive oil (for frying)

Boil, drain and mash the potatoes. While the potatoes are still hot, combine with minced beef, mortadella, egg, Parmesan and parsley. Season to taste with salt and pepper, and mix well with your hands. Shape into small logs or rissoles, and coat lightly in breadcrumbs.

Heat oil in a frying-pan (preferably non-stick), and fry rissoles for 4-6 minutes each side or until cooked through. Do not crowd the pan – fry in batches, if necessary. Remove and drain on paper towels. Serve immediately. ***Serves 4***

Handy tips

Meat: beef / veal / chicken

Italian rice croquettes

These croquettes are terrific as snacks or a light lunch. With all the added veggies, you could even get away with serving them on their own as a one-dish meal.

1 egg	¼ cup celery, finely chopped
125ml (½ cup) milk	½ cup frozen green peas
1 tbsp Parmesan cheese, grated	300g lean minced veal, beef or chicken
dry breadcrumbs (for coating)	2 cups cooked risotto (or white) rice
light olive oil (for frying)	25g (¼ cup) Parmesan cheese, grated
For the croquettes:	¼ cup flat-leaf parsley, finely chopped
small knob of butter	1 egg
1 tbsp extra-virgin olive oil	½ tsp salt (or to taste)
1 garlic clove, finely chopped	freshly ground black pepper
¼ cup onion, finely chopped	
¼ cup carrot, finely chopped	

To make the croquettes, heat butter and oil in a frying-pan over medium heat. Fry garlic, onion, carrot and celery until the vegetables soften. Stir in peas and cook briefly for about a minute. Remove from heat, and allow to cool slightly.

Combine minced meat with rice, cheese, parsley and egg. Add vegetables, and season with salt and pepper. Mix well using your hands. Shape into small logs of about 2cm thick, and 6-8 cm long. (Don't make them much longer or they will break easily.) Try and pack them tightly so that they will stay together during cooking.

> **Handy tips**
>
> **Meat**: veal / beef / chicken

Make the coating for the croquettes by beating egg with milk and cheese. Dip croquettes in egg-milk mixture, and then roll them in breadcrumbs. Heat oil in a frying-pan (preferably non-stick), and fry croquettes for 4-5 minutes each side or until meat is well cooked. Do not crowd the pan – fry in batches, if necessary. Remove from heat, and drain on paper towels. Serve immediately. ***Serves 3-4***

Medley of stuffed vegetables

Bursting with colours and flavours, this dish is 'delish', and certainly dinner-party worthy! It has so little meat in it that you could almost mistake it for a vegetarian dish.

100g (1 cup) basmati rice, uncooked	2 tbsp flat leaf parsley, finely chopped
4 medium capsicums (mix of red, green and yellow)	2 tbsp fresh chives (or tarragon), finely chopped
4 medium tomatoes	salt and freshly ground black pepper
4 medium onions, peeled	50g (½ cup) Parmesan cheese, grated
4-5 tbsp olive oil	
1-2 garlic cloves, finely chopped	1 egg yolk
200g lean minced beef or veal	

Cook rice in a large pan of salted water for about 8 minutes. Drain well and set aside.

Preheat oven to 200C (conventional). Wash and pat dry all the vegetables. Slice the tops off the capsicums about a-third of the way down, and reserve for later use. Discard seeds and membranes. (If any of the capsicums is not standing upright, cut a thin slice off its base).

Slice the tops off the tomatoes about a-third of the way down, scoop out the middle with a spoon, and reserve the tops and pulp for later use. Repeat this procedure with the onions. Then roughly chop the removed pulp of the tomatoes and onions.

> **Handy tips**
>
> **Meat**: beef / veal
>
> **How about** .. serving it on a bed of rocket or salad greens.

To make the stuffing, heat 2 tablespoons of oil in a frying-pan over medium heat. Add vegetable pulp and garlic to the pan, and fry until softened. Add minced beef, parsley and chives, and stir to combine, taking care to break up any lumps. Season with salt and pepper. Cover and cook for a few minutes. Remove from heat to a large bowl, and combine well with the cooked rice, Parmesan and egg yolk.

Fill vegetables with the stuffing, and put the tops back on all the vegetables. (Do not fill the vegetables to the brim as the rice expands during cooking.) Place in a baking tray, and brush with the remaining oil (2-3 tablespoons), pouring what is left into the tray. Bake in pre-heated oven for 35-40 minutes. ***Serves 4***

Stuffed cabbage leaves

There are literally dozens (if not hundreds) of wonderful recipes for stuffed cabbage leaves. I've chosen this one because of the toasted pine nuts, and the suggestion of peppers from the smoked paprika.

100g (2 rashers) bacon, finely chopped	¾ cup long-grain rice, cooked
1 onion, finely chopped	3 tbsp pine nuts, toasted
40g (2 tbsp) butter	2 tbsp fresh parsley, finely chopped
2 garlic cloves, crushed	1 tsp smoked paprika
1 tsp fresh thyme	salt and freshly ground black pepper
1 Savoy cabbage	400ml (1 ⅔ cups) tomato passata
500g lean minced beef	

Preheat oven to 180C (conventional), and grease a baking dish with a lid. Fry bacon and onion in butter over medium heat until onion softens. Add garlic and thyme, and fry for another minute. Remove from pan and set aside to cool.

Remove and discard tough, outer leaves from the cabbage. Cut leaves free from the core, and loosen each of the leaves (be careful to avoid tearing). You'd need about 8 leaves. Place cabbage leaves in a large pan of boiling water and cook for about 3 minutes. Drain and run them under a cold tap. Then drain well, and dry. (If you wish, you could cut about 1-2cm off the harder end of each cabbage leaf.)

> **Handy tips**
>
> **Meat**: beef
>
> **How about** .. serving it with mash (or even rice) and some buttered vegetables

Combine minced beef with the bacon/onion mixture, rice, pine nuts, parsley and paprika. Season with salt and pepper, and divide into 8 portions.

Lay out cabbage leaves on a flat surface. Spoon a portion of meat mixture onto each leaf, and roll up or wrap the cabbage leaf around it (folding in the sides). Repeat with remaining meat mixture and cabbage leaves.

Place cabbage rolls in the greased baking dish. Pour tomato passata on top. Cover with lid, and bake in pre-heated oven for 1 hour to 1¼ hours. ***Serves 4***

Stuffed zucchinis with tomato sauce

In Italy, every home cook would be armed with their variant of this recipe. You can understand why as they are delicious served hot or cold, and fare equally well as starters or main meals.

8 medium zucchinis

For the filling:

250g minced veal, beef or pork

25g (¼ cup) Parmesan cheese, grated

1 egg, lightly beaten

2 tbsp dry breadcrumbs

2 tbsp flat-leaf parsley, finely chopped

salt and freshly ground black pepper

For the tomato sauce:

2 tbsp olive oil

2 onions, finely chopped

1 large garlic clove, crushed

1 x 700g jar tomato passata

handful of basil leaves, torn

salt and freshly ground black pepper

Pre-heat oven to 180C (conventional), and grease a baking dish. Blanch whole zucchinis in salted, boiling water for 7-8 minutes or until just tender but not mushy. Drain and set aside to cool.

To make the filling, combine all ingredients and mix thoroughly.

Slice zucchinis in half lengthwise, and scoop or cut out the seeded core, reserving half of the removed pulp. Chop finely, and mix well with the meat filling. Then fill the zucchinis halves with this filling mixture. Place in the baking dish, and bake in pre-heated oven for about 25 minutes.

> **Handy tips**
>
> **Meat**: veal / beef / pork
>
> **How about** .. serving it with a plate of fluffy, white rice as a main meal

Meanwhile, make the tomato sauce by heating oil over medium heat. Add onions and garlic, and fry for several minutes until onions soften. Add tomato passata, basil, and season with salt and pepper. Cover and simmer for about 15 minutes.

Remove zucchinis from the oven, and pour the hot tomato sauce all over the top. Return to the oven and bake for a further 10 minutes. ***Serves 4***

Spinach meatballs in tomato sauce

These Spanish meatballs go particularly well with a spicy tomato sauce but you can serve them with a non-spicy sauce (just skip the cayenne pepper) or simply eat them on their own. Soft chorizos are available from select butchers. But if you can't find them, substitute with any spicy pork sausages.

For the meatballs:

1 bunch (about 250g) English spinach

500g minced pork (or pork mixed with beef, veal or lamb)

120g soft chorizos (or spicy pork sausages), skinned and crumbled

2 tbsp dry breadcrumbs

1 large egg, lightly beaten

pinch of grated nutmeg (optional)

salt and black pepper

plain flour (for coating)

olive oil (for frying)

For the tomato sauce:

olive oil

1 onion, finely chopped

1 x 400g tin chopped tomatoes

¼ cup dry sherry (or dry white wine)

1 bay leaf

¼ tsp paprika

pinch of cayenne pepper (optional)

salt (to taste)

To make the meatballs, bring a pan of salted water to a boil, and cook the spinach for 2-3 minutes. Drain and cool slightly. Then squeeze away excess water until as dry as possible, and chop finely. Combine with minced meat, chorizos, breadcrumbs, egg and nutmeg (if using). Season with salt and pepper, and mix well with your hands. Shape heaped tablespoons of the meat mixture into flat meatballs, and coat lightly in flour.

> ### *Handy tips*
>
> **Meat**: pork or pork & beef / veal / lamb
>
> **How about** .. serving them as starters, or with rice/mashed potatoes as a main meal.

To make the sauce, heat a little oil over medium heat. Add onion, and fry for several minutes until softened. Add tomatoes and bring to a boil. Allow it to bubble until the sauce thickens. Add sherry, bay leaf, paprika, cayenne pepper (if using), and salt. Reduce heat to low, and simmer, *uncovered,* for 10-15 minutes.

Meanwhile, in a non-stick frying-pan, heat oil over medium heat. Fry meatballs for about 5-6 minutes each side or until cooked through. Do not crowd the pan – fry in batches, if necessary. Serve with tomato sauce on the side. ***Serves 3-4***

123

Meatballs stuffed with apple and prune

This interesting recipe uses Asian spices but the cuisine is actually modern Scandinavian. Lightly sweetened with fruit, these luscious meatballs are simply delicious! If you don't want to add prunes, use one whole, red apple instead. The recipe requires a fair bit of milk which means that the mixture can be very sticky and even a bit runny.

½ **red apple (e.g. Red Delicious, Royal Gala), peeled and grated**

8 **prunes, pitted and chopped**

1 **tsp curry powder**

60ml (¼ **cup) water**

600g **minced pork**

160ml (⅔ **cup) milk**

2 **tbsp plain flour**

¼ **tsp grated nutmeg**

¼ **tsp ground ginger**

½ **tsp salt (or to taste)**

butter (for frying)

To make the stuffing, place apple, prunes, curry powder and water in a small pan. Bring to a boil, and reduce heat to low. Simmer gently until it turns into a thick paste. Stir occasionally and add a little more water, if necessary. Remove from heat, and set aside to cool.

Combine minced pork with milk, flour, nutmeg, ginger and salt. Mix well using your hands. (If you wish to check seasoning, fry a small lump of meat mixture – taste and adjust.) Cover and refrigerate for 1 hour or more. (The mixture will stiffen a little with refrigeration but if it is still too sticky, knead it briefly for 30 seconds or so with your hands.)

> **Handy tips**
>
> **Meat**: pork
>
> **How about** .. serving them with mashed potatoes and coleslaw

Divide the meat mixture into 10-12 portions. With the back of a spoon, flatten a portion of meat mixture into about 5cm (diameter). Spoon a little prune/apple stuffing into the centre, and fold the meat mixture around the stuffing to make a flat meatball. (You may wish to moisten your hands for easier handling of meat mixture.) Repeat this with the remaining meat mixture and stuffing.

In a non-stick frying-pan, heat butter over medium heat. Fry meatballs for 5-6 minutes each side or until cooked through. Do not crowd the pan – fry in batches, if necessary. Remove from pan and drain on paper towels. Serve immediately. ***Serves 3-4***

Baked meatballs

This is a Swedish recipe. As these meatballs are baked, they are easy to prepare, and handy as a starter if your friends are coming over – just prepare them ahead, store in the fridge, and pop them in the oven when your guests arrive. I put in fresh dill to add interest but if you're not a big fan of the feathery herb, feel free to leave it out – the meatballs will still be as tender and moist!

1 slice sandwich bread, crumbed (or 3 tbsps dry breadcrumbs)

2 tbsp pouring cream (or milk)

2 tbsp water

500g minced beef (or ½ beef, ½ veal/pork)

1 small onion, finely chopped

1 tbsp fresh dill, finely chopped

1 egg, lightly beaten

1 tsp salt (or to taste)

¼ tsp freshly ground black pepper

Preheat oven to 200C (conventional), and grease a baking tray or line it with baking paper. Soak breadcrumbs in cream and water for 10 minutes or more.

Combine breadcrumb mixture with minced meat, onion, dill, and egg. Season with salt and black pepper. Using your hands, mix until ingredients are *just* combined. Do not overwork the mixture if you want the meatballs to be light in texture. (If you wish to check seasoning, fry a small lump of meat mixture – taste and adjust.)

Shape level tablespoons of meat mixture into balls, and place on the baking tray. Bake in pre-heated oven for 10 minutes. Then turn them over once, and bake for a further 10 minutes.
Serves 5-6 as a starter; Serves 3-4 as a main meal

> ### Handy tips
>
> **Meat**: beef or beef & veal / pork
>
> **How about** .. serving them with mashed potatoes, and a cooked vegetable dish like ratatouille, if you're serving them as a main meal

Kotlety in sour cream sauce

These are oval-shaped meat patties from the Russian cuisine. In this recipe, egg whites are beaten until stiffened and then folded into the meat mixture, resulting in tender and succulent patties! The mixture is a little sticky so you may wish to moisten your hands with cold water for easier handling.

1 slice sandwich bread (white or wholemeal)

250ml (1 cup) beef stock

600g lean minced beef

2 eggs, separated

butter (1 tbsp melted, plus extra for frying)

¼ tsp salt (or to taste)

freshly ground black pepper

plain flour (for coating)

160ml (²/₃ cup) sour cream

Soak bread in one-third of the stock (¹/₃ cup) for 10 minutes, and squeeze away excess liquid. Combine bread mixture with minced beef, egg yolks and melted butter, and season with salt and pepper. Mix with your hands until ingredients are just combined. Do not overwork the mixture if you want the kotlety to be light in texture.

Beat egg whites until peaks start to form, and gently fold into the meat mixture. (If you wish to check seasoning, fry a small lump of meat mixture – taste and adjust.) Shape into kotlety or oval-shaped patties (about 5-6 cm wide), and coat lightly in flour.

In a non-stick frying-pan, quickly fry kotlety in butter until lightly browned all over. Do not crowd the pan – fry in batches, if necessary. Remove from pan, and drain on paper towels.

In the pan you've used to fry the kotlety, add sour cream, and the remaining beef stock (²/₃ cup). Stir to mix well with the meat juices. Then return kotlety to the pan. Simmer, *uncovered*, for about 10 minutes or until cooked through. ***Serves 4***

Handy tips

Meat: beef

How about .. serving them with boiled potatoes and peas. Baked cabbage also goes well with this dish. Take ½ a shredded cabbage, add 2 tbsp water and simmer it, covered, for 5 minutes. Add 2 chopped tomatoes (peeled), 3 tbsp stock and seasoning, and simmer for another 10 minutes. Place cabbage mixture in oven proof dish, and cover it with 2 thinly sliced tomatoes. Brush the top with oil, and bake in pre-heated oven (180C conventional) for about 30 minutes.

Baked Scotch eggs

These Scotch eggs are baked in a muffin tin rather than deep fried, making them healthier and easier to prepare than their traditional counterparts. You can use sausage meat or sausages that are made from a variety of meats (pork, beef or chicken) to suit your taste preference. They can be eaten either hot or cold, and are terrific for school lunches and picnics.

12 large (or medium) hard-boiled eggs, shelled

4 slices sandwich bread (white or wholemeal), crusts removed

180ml (¾ cup) milk

1 kg good quality sausage meat (or sausages, skinned and crumbled)

1 small onion, finely chopped

2 tbsp fresh parsley, finely chopped

1 egg, lightly beaten

black pepper

Preheat oven to 190C (conventional), and lightly grease a 12-hole muffin tin.

Soak bread in milk for about 10 minutes. Squeeze away excess liquid. Add the bread mixture to the sausage meat, onion, parsley, egg and black pepper. Mix well using your hands.

Press a little meat mixture into the bottom of a hole in the muffin tin. Place an egg with its pointy end facing up, and pack the meat mixture around and over it, covering it completely. Repeat this with the remaining meat mixture and eggs.

Bake in pre-heated oven for 25 minutes or until browned. Allow to stand for 10 minutes in the tin before serving. ***Makes 12***

> ### Handy tips
>
> **Meat**: pork / beef / chicken / veal
>
> **How about** .. adding ½ cup grated cheese to the meat mixture for variation

Butternut pumpkin and meatballs

This is a fabulous recipe from contemporary Australian cuisine. Pumpkin has a sweetish taste and a velvety texture that many kids love so this dish will go down well with the little ones. If you don't have a food processor or meat/spice grinder, simply chop all the ingredients for meatballs finely, and combine them well with your hands.

2 tbsp olive oil

1 red capsicum, seeded and chopped

1 large onion, chopped

2 garlic cloves, crushed

1 tsp fresh thyme

1 small butternut pumpkin, peeled, seeded and cut into small cubes

salt and black pepper

1 tbsp fresh mint, chopped (optional)

For the meatballs:

500g minced beef

1 medium onion, finely chopped

1 clove garlic, crushed

2 tbsp fresh coriander leaves, finely chopped

2 tsp ground cumin

1 tsp ground coriander

½ tsp salt (or to taste)

½ tsp black pepper

olive oil (for frying)

For the meatballs, combine all ingredients (except oil), and mix well using your hands. Cover and refrigerate for 1 hour or more. Shape tablespoons of meat mixture into balls. In a frying-pan (preferably non-stick) with a lid to fit, quickly fry meatballs until browned all over. Do not crowd the pan –fry in batches, if necessary. Drain on paper towels, and set aside. Clean the pan.

Heat oil in the pan over medium heat. Add capsicum, onion, garlic and thyme, and fry for several minutes until the onion is soft but not browned. Then add pumpkin, and cook for 10 minutes, stirring frequently to prevent sticking.

Return meatballs to the pan, and turn heat to low. Cover and cook for another 20 minutes. Season with salt and pepper. Sprinkle with mint, and serve immediately. ***Serves 4***

> ### *Handy tips*
> **Meat**: beef
>
> **How about** .. serving it with warm pita bread, salad and tzatziki or Greek-style yoghurt

Cottage pie

Many of us would have a favourite recipe for this comforting dish! If you don't, why not give this one a try? It doesn't require any tinned tomatoes – only a little tomato paste. This gives it a point of difference from other recipes that are more heavily tomato-based.

1-2 tbsp olive oil	330ml (1 $\frac{1}{3}$ cups) beef (or vegetable) stock
1 garlic clove, crushed	
1 large onion, finely chopped	1 tbsp Worcestershire sauce
500g minced beef or lamb	1 tbsp tomato paste
1 celery stalk, finely chopped	500g potatoes, quartered
1 carrot, finely chopped	80ml ($\frac{1}{3}$ cup) milk
75g (½ cup) frozen green peas (optional)	30g (1½ tbsp) butter or margarine
	handful of grated cheese

Heat oil over medium-high heat, and add garlic and onion. Fry for several minutes or until onion softens and browns lightly. Add minced meat and fry for another few minutes until browned, taking care to break up any lumps. Add celery, carrot and peas (if using). Fry vegetables for 3-4 minutes, stirring frequently. Add stock, Worcestershire sauce and tomato paste. Stir to combine and bring to a boil. Turn heat to low, and simmer, *uncovered*, for 20-25 minutes or until the mixture is quite *dry*, stirring occasionally.

> **Handy tips**
>
> **Meat**: beef / lamb
>
> **How about** .. adding a handful of fresh herbs (oregano, thyme or rosemary) when you're frying the carrot and peas

Preheat oven to 200C (conventional). In a pan, boil potatoes until tender. Drain, and mash with milk and butter.

Spread meat mixture over the bottom of a baking dish, and cover with mashed potatoes. Sprinkle cheese evenly on top. Bake in pre-heated oven for 25-30 minutes or until the top is lightly golden. ***Serves 4***

Cottage pie with a twist

This recipe uses cauliflower instead of potatoes, and may seem a little unusual at first glance. But the cauliflower actually ends up tasting like yummy mash – only much lighter. Make sure you don't overcook the cauliflower and spend a couple of minutes drying it out as suggested.

1 medium cauliflower, cut into large florets	**1 tbsp plain flour**
	½ x 400g tin chopped tomatoes
2 tbsp plain yoghurt	**250ml (1 cup) stock (beef, chicken or vegetable)**
1 egg yolk	
salt and freshly ground black pepper	**2 bay leaves (optional)**
4 tbsp olive oil	**1 tsp fresh thyme**
500g lean minced beef	**2 tsp Worcestershire sauce**
1 large onion, finely chopped	**2 tbsp cheddar cheese, grated**

Place cauliflower in a large pot of salted boiling water. Cover and simmer over low heat for about 15 minutes until tender but not mushy. Drain and return to pot for a couple of minutes. (The heat of the pot will dry out the cauliflower even more.) Shake the pot a few times to prevent cauliflower from sticking. Place cauliflower in a blender or food processor, and blend until smooth. Empty into a bowl, and whisk in yoghurt and egg yolk. Season with salt and pepper.

Preheat oven to 180C (conventional). In a frying-pan, heat half the olive oil (2 tablespoons) over medium-high heat, and fry minced beef until browned and *dry*, taking care to break up any lumps. Remove from pan, and set aside. Clean the pan.

Add the remaining olive oil (2 tablespoons) to the pan, and turn heat to low. Fry onion for 6-8 minutes until soft but not browned. Add flour, and stir to mix well. Then add tomatoes, stock, bay leaves (if using), thyme and Worcestershire sauce, and bring to a boil. Simmer gently, *uncovered*, for about 10 minutes or until mixture is quite *dry*, stirring occasionally. Discard bay leaves (if using), and return minced beef to the pan.

> **Handy tips**
>
> **Meat**: beef
>
> **How about** ..
> serving it with buttered peas or steamed greens

Put meat mixture into a baking dish, and cover it with the mashed cauliflower. Smooth over the top with a knife or spatula, and finish off with an even sprinkling of grated cheese. Bake in pre-heated oven for 25-30 minutes. ***Serves 4***

Cuban picadillo

Olives and green capsicum make perfect partners in this Cuban version of picadillo, and give the dish its distinctive flavour. It is easy to prepare, and you can turn it into a one-pot meal by adding more potatoes.

olive oil	3 garlic cloves, crushed
2 potatoes, cut into small cubes	2 tbsp green olives, pitted and chopped
1 large onion, chopped	
1 large green capsicum, seeded and chopped	60ml (¼ cup) red wine
	1 tbsp vinegar
500g minced beef	salt and black pepper
3 tomatoes, roughly chopped	

In a frying-pan (preferably non-stick) with a lid to fit, heat oil over medium heat Fry potatoes for a few minutes or until lightly browned. Remove and set aside. Clean the pan.

Heat a little more oil in the pan, and fry onion and green capsicum for 2-3 minutes or until vegetables soften. Add minced beef, tomatoes and garlic, and fry until meat browns, taking care to break up any lumps. Return potatoes to the pan, and add olives, wine and vinegar. Season with salt and pepper. Cover and simmer over low heat for about 30 minutes or until potatoes are cooked.
Serves 4

> **Handy tips**
>
> **Meat**: beef
>
> **How about** .. serving it with rice or bread.

Cuban meatballs in tomato sauce

These albondigas are lovely, tender meatballs cooked in a tomato sauce flavoured with green capsicum! You'd need slightly less than half a packet of plain cracker biscuits for crumbing in a food processor or meat/spice grinder. But if you don't have the means for crumbing biscuits, use three tablespoons of dried breadcrumbs instead.

For the meatballs:

500g minced beef

½ cup cracker biscuit crumbs

60ml (¼ cup) milk

1 egg

1 small onion, finely chopped

2-3 spring onions, finely chopped

1 tsp ground cumin

1 tsp dried oregano (optional)

½ tsp salt (or to taste)

¼ tsp black pepper

plain flour (for coating)

olive oil (for frying)

For the tomato sauce:

1 tbsp olive oil

1 large onion, chopped

1 large green capsicum, seeded and chopped

3-4 garlic cloves, crushed

1 x 700g jar tomato passata

1 tbsp white vinegar

2-3 tsp brown sugar

¼ tsp salt (or to taste)

To make the meatballs, combine all ingredients (except flour and oil), and mix well with your hands. Shape heaped tablespoons of meat mixture into balls, and coat them lightly in flour. In a frying-pan, (preferably non-stick), with a lid to fit, heat oil over medium heat, and quickly fry meatballs until lightly browned all over. Do not crowd the pan – fry this in batches, if necessary. Remove meatballs from pan, and set aside.

To make the sauce, heat oil in the pan you used to fry the meatballs. Fry onion and green capsicum for a few minutes until softened. Add garlic, and fry for 1-2 minutes. Then stir in tomato passata, vinegar, sugar and salt. Return meatballs to the pan, and bring sauce to a boil before reducing heat to low. Cover and simmer for about 30 minutes, turning meatballs over occasionally to coat them evenly with sauce.

Serves 3-4

> **Handy tips**
>
> **Meat**: beef
>
> **How about** .. serving it with white rice or even pasta

Mexican picadillo

The list of ingredients for this recipe may be long but the preparation is really easy! It freezes well, and can be used as a filling for a whole host of dishes such as tortillas, tacos, enchiladas, and empanadas. It's essentially a version of chilli beef, and although it doesn't use any beans, it is just as delicious! The sultanas are a nice touch if you like a little fruitiness mixed in with spiciness. If you don't, just leave them out.

2 tbsp vegetable oil

1 large onion, finely chopped

2 garlic cloves, crushed

700g minced beef or pork

4 large tomatoes, peeled and chopped

1-2 jalapeno peppers, sliced

½ cup sultanas (optional)

2 tbsp red wine (or regular) vinegar

2 tbsp tomato paste

3 tsp chilli powder (or to taste)

1 tsp ground coriander

1 tsp ground cinnamon

1 tsp ground cumin

½ tsp ground allspice

salt and black pepper

Heat oil in a large pan over medium-high heat. Add onion and garlic, and fry for several minutes until onion browns. Add minced meat, and fry until browned, taking care to break up any lumps. Then add all the remaining ingredients, and turn heat to low. Cover and simmer gently for 30 minutes. If the mixture dries out, add a little water. Serve immediately. ***Serves 4-5***

Handy tips

Meat: beef / pork

How about .. frying ¼ cup slivered almonds in a little oil, and sprinkle them over the picadillo. This dish also goes nicely over whole baked potatoes if you're looking for a change

Index

Author's Background

The author, Nancy Chan Bennett is Chinese-Australian, and was born and raised in Hong Kong. After graduation, she spent two years in Papua New Guinea where she had to quickly learn to cook. She came to Sydney in 1977, and spent many years in market research and marketing before training as a teacher. She has lived and travelled extensively, particularly in Asia, and benefited from all the taste sensations associated with various cultures. While she has never received any professional training in cooking (except for a short course in French cake-making), her interest in cooking and love of food has continued to keep her firmly focused on the pursuit of new culinary tastes and sensations.